The Alaska

HOMESTEADER'S HANDBOOK

Independent Living on the Last Frontier

Tricia Brown and Nancy Gates

ALASKA
NORTHWEST
BOOKS®

To honor my grandma, and hers.
—T. B.

To Betty Talley Neal, my mother, mentor, and friend.
—N. G.

Text © 2012 by Tricia Brown and Nancy Gates.
Photos © 2012 to various photographers as credited.

Front cover photo credits, clockwise from top left: Roy Corral; Joe Doner; Ray Williams; © iStockphoto.com/
Bart Coenders; © iStockphoto.com/Beverley Vycital; Lynette Clark. Front and back cover border: © iStock-
photo.com/Alexander Chernyakov.
p. 77, highbush cranberry: iStock/Pi-Lens; p. 78, currant: iStock/masselsa; blueberry: iStock/Jurate; juneberry:
iStock/Murphy_Shewchuk; bog cranberry: iStock/intst; lowbush cranberry: iStock/MHjerpe.

Library of Congress Cataloging-in-Publication Data

Brown, Tricia.
The Alaska homesteader's handbook : independent living on the last frontier / by Tricia Brown
    and Nancy Gates.
      p. cm.
Includes bibliographical references and index.
 ISBN 978-0-88240-811-8 (pbk.)
 ISBN 978-0-88240-917-7 (e-book)
1. Self-reliant living—Alaska. 2. Sustainable living—Alaska. 3. Wilderness
survival—Alaska. 4. Alaska—Social life and customs. I. Gates, Nancy. II. Title.
GF78.B76 2012
613.6'909798—dc23

                          2012024105

Cover and interior design: Vicki Knapton
Illustrations: Natalie Gates

Alaska Northwest Books® An imprint of

GRAPHIC ARTS
BOOKS®

P.O. Box 56118
Portland, OR 97238-6118
(503) 254-5591

www.graphicartsbooks.com

Settlers on the Last Frontier

Numbers correspond to chapters

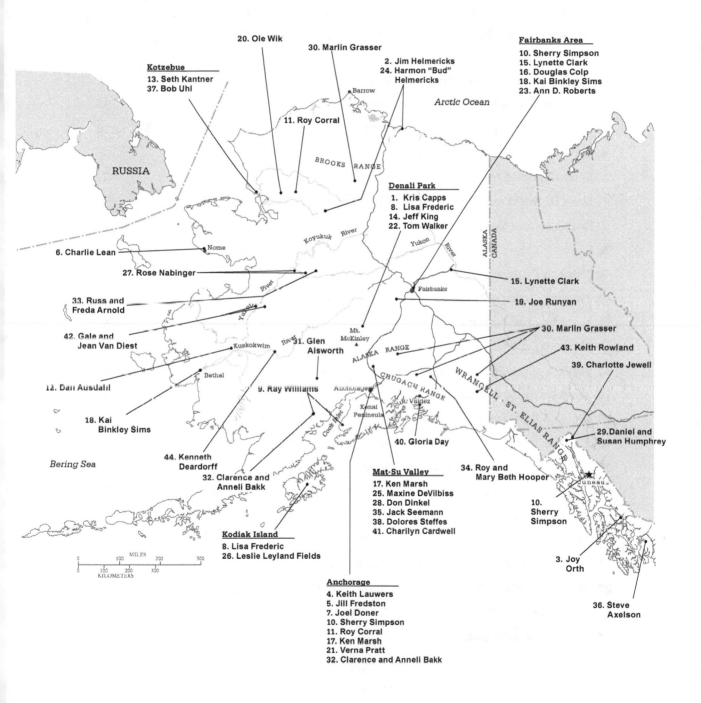

20. Ole Wik

30. Marlin Grasser

2. Jim Helmericks
24. Harmon "Bud"
    Helmericks

Fairbanks Area
10. Sherry Simpson
15. Lynette Clark
16. Douglas Colp
18. Kai Binkley Sims
23. Ann D. Roberts

Kotzebue
13. Seth Kantner
37. Bob Uhl

11. Roy Corral

Barrow

Arctic Ocean

RUSSIA

BROOKS RANGE

Denali Park
1. Kris Capps
8. Lisa Frederic
14. Jeff King
22. Tom Walker

Koyukuk River

Yukon River

ALASKA
CANADA

6. Charlie Lean

Nome

15. Lynette Clark

27. Rose Nabinger

Fairbanks

19. Joe Runyan

33. Russ and
    Freda Arnold

River

30. Marlin Grasser

42. Gale and
    Jean Van Diest

Yukon

Mt.
McKinley

43. Keith Rowland

39. Charlotte Jewell

Kuskokwim

River

**31. Glen
Alsworth**

ALASKA RANGE

WRANGELL · ST. ELIAS RANGE

12. Dan Ausdahl

Bethel

9. Ray Williams

Anchorage

CHUGACH RANGE

18. Kai
    Binkley Sims

Valdez

29. Daniel and
    Susan Humphrey

Bering Sea

Kenai
Peninsula

Juneau

40. Gloria Day

10.
Sherry
Simpson

44. Kenneth
    Deardorff

Cook Inlet

**34. Roy and
Mary Beth Hooper**

32. Clarence and
    Anneli Bakk

Mat-Su Valley
17. Ken Marsh
25. Maxine DeVilbiss
28. Don Dinkel
35. Jack Seemann
38. Dolores Steffes
41. Charilyn Cardwell

MILES
0   100   200   300

0   100   200   300
KILOMETERS

Kodiak Island
8. Lisa Frederic
26. Leslie Leyland Fields

3. Joy
   Orth

**36. Steve
Axelson**

Anchorage
4. Keith Lauwers
5. Jill Fredston
7. Joel Doner
10. Sherry Simpson
11. Roy Corral
17. Ken Marsh
21. Verna Pratt
32. Clarence and Anneli Bakk

CONTENTS

"The greatest thing you'll ever meet in Alaska is yourself."

Harmon "Bud" Helmericks paused for a formal photo on the day he flew solo to the North Pole in his Cessna 170, around 1950. He signed this print as a gift for his son Jim in 1956. *(Photo courtesy Jim Helmericks Family)*

Foreword • Proving Up the Alaska Way

Alaska has always had a freedom that other states—and countries—don't have. And you can't explain freedom to someone who's never really known it. Some people have a spirit of adventure—a very few—and some don't. Most don't. Most wouldn't do anything different if given the chance.

I was born in 1917, so I was twenty-three years old when I came to Alaska from Champaign, Illinois. I never "first came up." I came up to stay in 1940. (During the Depression, you didn't go very far to "visit" anybody.) My great-uncle Fred had been a signal corpsman with the US Army Corps of Engineers in Seward. I got my opinions of Alaska from him; he loved Alaska and spent his life here.

So, the first place I came to was Seward. I worked for the railroad—that was the only work there really was. My job was transferring freight—groceries, supplies, anything you shipped up in those days—from the steamships to railroad cars bound for Anchorage and Fairbanks.

Later I settled on the Arctic Coast and explored all over the North Slope and Canada by dog team and Bush plane . . . for discovery. It was like, "The bear went over the mountain to see what he could see." And I've flown over more pack ice than most people ever dream of. Of course, folks in the Lower 48 never did have to fly—with roads all over. For us in Alaska, roads sort of spoiled the country.

Alaska always fascinates people. But if you don't like your wife or your husband, don't think going to Alaska will solve that problem. Just forget it. Don't waste your money. If you don't both have an adventurous spirit, and are willing to carry it through, don't think Alaska's going to fix your problems in life. You'll take them with you.

It's a big job [living in the wilderness]. You have to be willing to tighten your belt. Don't think Alaska's going to pay your bills, financial or otherwise. You've got to pay your own way. Alaska wants anybody who's willing to carry his own burdens, anyone who's willing to give more than 100 percent. You've got to be willing to work twice as hard as other people, and be self-sufficient.

And don't blame others for your problems. You have to bump your own head. When you open that cupboard door, and you rise up under it, you know it's not the first time, and it's not the fault of the carpenter who put the door there. You've got to be practical. You know, practicality is kind of scarce.

The greatest thing you'll ever meet in Alaska is yourself. It's an awfully pretty spot that gives you a chance to really live life. Martha and I are so grateful [for our time in the Arctic]. In fact, we're still there—in spirit.

It's home. It will always be home.

—Harmon "Bud" Helmericks, July 2008
Colville Village, Walker Lake, and Fairbanks, Alaska

Introduction • The Book of Experience

Just what kind of person decides to go North and build a life in the Last Frontier? Throughout Alaska's history, restless adventurers have made their way here, as have gold seekers, outdoor enthusiasts, and poets. The military "invited" a lot of people. So did Big Oil and other employers. Some have arrived to start a new life—or to escape the old one; others are lucky enough to be born here. It all makes for an interesting mix in the population. So you might be sitting on a plane, waiting for a bus, or at the doctor's office, and strike up a casual conversation with somebody who turns out to be a truly extraordinary individual. You find one who headed North against incredible odds, and through strength, intelligence, tenacity—and sometimes just dumb luck—etched out a rewarding life in the wilds of this rugged, unforgettable, unforgiving, achingly gorgeous land. If you get this person talking, and if you really listen, you'll come away wiser.

And now you're about to gain from the experiences of more than forty pioneer types we interviewed for the *The Alaska Homesteader's Handbook*. We tracked them down and asked each one for a helpful piece of advice, some tip or instruction on getting along in the wilderness. Some were actual homesteaders or had grown up on a remote site; others moved in and out of the Bush seasonally. By genetic predisposition or by hard-won experience (or both), all had acquired how-to that set them apart. They're old and young, male and female, Bush-dweller and city folk, first-generation to fourth-generation Alaskans. What they have in common is the pursuit of their Alaska dream.

For the elders, talking with us brought back rich memories of a life they'd return to in a heartbeat if time and strength would allow it. The younger ones are strong and sure and chasing their dream, still loving the place that at times seems hell-bent on killing them.

As we got to know them, we found the type who have great stories, but tend to sit on them. You know these kinds. They're thinking, "What's all the fuss? You do what you have to do." As if any of us could cut up a 55-gallon drum and fashion a homemade woodstove, or make a dock out of logs and boxes of rocks. Others were natural-born storytellers, and some of their tales seemed made for TV: sitting up in a sleeping bag and shooting a couple of rounds out the tent flap to get rid of a nosy bear; washing the gold miners' work clothes, then panning the mud at the bottom of the wringer washer for gold; reusing baby's bath water three ways before pouring it on the garden.

These aren't dusty stories from history books. We interviewed real people of all ages and from all walks of life—from the gold miner who was still digging at age ninety-four to the twenty-something female riverboat captain. We talked to descendants of 1930s New Deal colonists, military people who stuck around after discharge, and pipeline pioneers of the 1970s. We found folks who wanted to escape materialism and others who just wanted to discover what they could do, adventure-seekers in the purest sense. They settled all over the land, in every region of the territory that became America's forty-ninth state in 1959.

Alaska was still under Russian rule when President Abraham Lincoln signed the Homestead Act of 1862. Suddenly, average Americans were given a phenomenal opportunity: to become landowners. As long as the applicant was head of the household, at least twenty-one, and had never borne arms against the United States, he or she qualified. For the first time in history, former slaves, new immigrants, and unmarried women were on equal footing with white men. They could acquire patent for up to 160 acres by "proving up": living on it for five years, improving it, and farming a portion. Fees totaled less than $20. Or, if a homesteader lived on the property for six months, there was the option to purchase it outright for $1.25 per acre. After the United States purchased Alaska from Russia in 1867, homesteading opened in the Far North, too, and settlers trickled in during the early and mid-twentieth century.

Homesteading rules changed over time, and during the life of the law, more than 270 million acres were homesteaded across the country. By 1976, the federal homesteading program was repealed in the Lower 48, but a special exemption for Alaska extended land selection until 1986.

As it happens, the very last federal homestead in America was staked in Alaska. Kenneth Deardorff's parcel on the Stony River was the last to receive patent before the federal government closed a door that a Civil War president had opened. You'll find his story in the last chapter of *The Alaska Homesteader's Handbook*, where he offers sound advice on how to survive an Alaska winter in a tent.

While homesteading isn't permitted anymore, not even on the Last Frontier, various state programs offer public land—usually way-out-there land—for purchase through the Department of Natural Resources. Some programs are for Alaskans only; others are open to anyone.

Ask the settlers in this book. Homesteading is not solely about staking a claim. It's about staking your Alaska dream. And dreams will always be free.

—Tricia Brown,
Alaskan, 1978–1999

—Nancy Gates,
Alaskan since 1978

1 How to Live Off the Grid

KRIS CAPPS, Denali Park
Alaskan since 1980

During the 1980s, Illinois native Kris Capps covered the cops-and-courts beat for the *Fairbanks Daily News-Miner*, reporting daily on crime—some seriously evil, some plain comical. There was the man who was shot by his dog. There was the raid of the marijuana field that turned out to be potatoes. And the drunken man who drove his airboat down the highway. She also covered the story of Christopher McCandless, whose solitary death in an abandoned bus was fodder for a best-selling book and movie titled *Into the Wild*. And in the "stranger than fiction" category, Kris covered a murder investigation, dutifully submitting her stories to her editor, and later learned he was in fact hiding the murderer.

With help from friends, Kris and her former husband built their first Denali Park cabin in 1986.
(Photo courtesy Kris Capps)

"I was always amazed that people in my town could do those things," Kris says. "I'm basically an optimistic person, and I didn't realize how much it weighed on me until after I left."

On the side, Kris led wild river expeditions in the Brooks Range, and taught kayaking to innumerable students. Camping and paddling in the wilderness was a balm as well as an escape from the realities of crime reporting.

After a decade at the newspaper, Kris joined her then-husband at their home site just outside Denali National Park, a two-acre parcel they'd acquired through a state lottery program offered to Alaskans for a $35 filing fee and the cost of surveying. They built a small cabin in 1986 with help from friends. The couple lived without electricity and running water, but soon developed a workable system.

There in her snug home, Kris continued to write for publications throughout the country, including a year's worth of assignments from *People* magazine.

"I'm sitting in my little cabin with my slippers on, under my propane lights, and talking to someone who's obviously in some fancy office in New York," she remembers. "You look around and say, 'If they only knew.'"

What they didn't know: their professional correspondent lived in a 16-by-16 cabin in the Alaska Range, not far from America's tallest peak, the 20,320-foot Mount McKinley. She used a computer and modem powered by batteries that were charged with solar panels or a wind generator. Neither solar nor wind power were useful during the darkest, dead calm winter months, however, so her backup was the gas-powered generator. There was propane for lighting and refrigeration, an oil stove for heat, and water that the couple hauled in five-gallon jugs. The outhouse was out back. And each bitterly cold morning, a couple of hours before the "commute" to work, one of them had to rise and fire up the generator so they could plug in the car to thaw the motor oil.

"When you're doing it, you don't think about it, you just do it," Kris says. "I'd have friends come down in the summer when it was a glorious day, and they'd say, 'Oh you're so lucky!' But sometimes I didn't feel so lucky in the middle of winter when it was 35 below zero, and it was dark, and I couldn't get the generator started."

As for bathing, because Kris's husband was a National Park Service employee, they had the option of showering at a park facility, but that was twenty miles round-trip. It was either drive or take a sponge bath.

"You just get used to it, and it doesn't seem that unusual," Kris says. "But it does teach you how to conserve water."

In the early 1990s, the couple built what Kris calls a "real" house in the same area. It has a spacious floor plan, spectacular views of the Alaska Range, and water that comes out of a tap. But don't be fooled—the plumbing is connected to a 500-gallon tank in the basement.

"I still haul water 180 gallons at a time in the back of a truck, and that's fine except when it's 35

During a visit to McCarthy, Kris uses a solar-powered public phone to check on flight arrangements into Wrangell-St. Elias National Park and Preserve. *(Photo by Tricia Brown)*

below," says Kris. She's quick to laugh at her over-vigilance when dinner guests offer to wash up. "People who don't have to conserve water, your stomach just tightens when they're at your house. They fill the entire sink! I could probably get three loads of dishes done with that."

In 1995, Kris and her neighbors were offered the option of joining the commercial power grid. A few declined, but Kris was ready, especially as a new mother.

"Things change, you get older, you have a family," she reflects.

Without question, life is easier, albeit more expensive, on the grid. But it's allowed Kris to stay right where she wants to be—living and working virtually in the shadow of Mount McKinley. ■

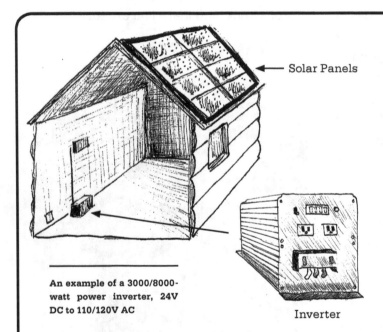

Solar Panels

An example of a 3000/8000-watt power inverter, 24V DC to 110/120V AC

Inverter

HOUSEHOLD USES FOR AC

Energy from solar panels is stored in direct current (DC) batteries. You connect the battery to an inverter, which changes it to conventional alternating current (AC), for most household uses. You can plug your AC devices directly into the inverter, or include the inverter as part of the household wiring, so you can plug in anywhere. Consult a solar power expert to determine your power needs. You can purchase the panels, batteries, and inverter, plus all connecting cable in a package that will work for you.

Motorists in the North plug in their engine-block heaters a couple of hours before starting a car when temperatures drop below zero, warming the motor oil and saving wear and tear on the components. In deepest cold, sometimes a battery blanket or oil-pan heater is advised as well.

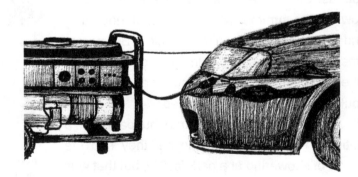

2 How to Dress for Below-Zero Temps

JIM HELMERICKS, Colville Village
Alaskan since 1953

Jim Helmericks raised his family along the Arctic Ocean, where his pioneering parents built a family enclave called Colville Village. Where polar bears roam and the nearest real town is Barrow, "America's farthest-north city," about ninety minutes away by small plane. And where the wind chill can get down to -100°F. All across Alaska's North Slope, residents are wise to take care in how they bundle up before going outside. To do otherwise is to risk their very lives.

So the question that Jim gets most often is: *Why? Why do you live here?*

His simple answer: "Because I love the country. You learn to live with it. It kind of grows on you."

Jim was a boy in 1956 when his aviator-author father, Harmon "Bud" Helmericks, was running his Arctic Tern Fish & Freight Co. from their remote Walker Lake cabin in the Brooks Range. Colville Village was their fishing site then, but over time Colville grew from a smattering of tents to a frame home, a hangar, and other outbuildings.

"At first we moved from place to place as the season dictated," Jim remembers. June was fishing at Walker Lake. In July, it was the coast for commercial fishing, and then on to Barrow for walrus hunting. Fall was guiding hunters at Walker Lake and on the Arctic Coast. Then back to Colville for early winter commercial fishing. In the spring came polar-bear hunting. Jim helped by refueling planes, moving gear, and taking care of the trophies when they returned home. Until the mid-1960s, the family also traveled for Bud's lecture tours.

"We'd hit almost every state in the Lower 48. Dad lectured

Above: Teena and Jim raised Derek, Jay, and Isaac at the top of the world, adopting many of the cold-weather skills practiced by their Native Alaskan neighbors.

Right: In this photo from the late 1960s, Jim's exhaled breath quickly turns to frost on eyelashes and a parka's wolf ruff. *(Photos courtesy Jim Helmericks)*

and we lived out of a car for about four months," Jim says. "Then we'd get back up for polar-bear guiding in the spring."

Jim's mother homeschooled her sons (one of whom became a Rhodes Scholar), and all three learned about the Arctic and aviation from the ground up. The Helmericks family was already present when the oilfield in Prudhoe Bay was discovered and played an invaluable role in support services and as environmental consultants, and one Helmericks son still does.

In 1970, Jim married Teena, who'd grown up in Barrow, the daughter of family friends. So moving to tree-less Colville Village posed little adjustment. They raised four boys and worked together guiding, commercial fishing, and operating an air taxi. All four of their homeschooled sons went on to graduate from college and continue to live in Alaska.

Jim and Teena are grandparents now. Their house is still heated with wood—but not collected driftwood as in the old days. "Most of our wood is square-sided anymore," Jim jokes. They get it from their nearest neighbors, the oilfields. He and Teena have made a museum of their extensive collection of Arctic memorabilia, mounted wildlife, and Native artifacts. They host visitors from around the world—scientists to laymen—who often come when bird-watching is at its best. Their home also happens to lie on a major migratory bird flyway.

"We have the largest brant colony on the North Slope spread out within two miles of the

Above: In 1970, Jim's baby was a Super Cub, here outfitted with oversized tires for ease in landing on remote airstrips. *(Photo courtesy Jim Helmericks)*

Left: Teena Helmericks and son Isaac pose with their pet caribou, Clyde. *(Photo courtesy Jim Helmericks)*

house, with nesting pairs all the way up to our doorstep," Jim says. "We have a lot of birds. You step outside; it's just a symphony of birdsongs and calls. All of a sudden fall comes and you step outside and it's quiet. 'Uh-oh, winter's coming.'

"To me it doesn't seem that out of the ordinary. It's hard to come up with what people think are good stories, for me. This is just my life."

From a lifetime of experience, Teena offers the following advice on how to stay warm when the temperature drops below zero. ∎

Staying Warm

COLD IN THE ARCTIC is different from cold in other places in Alaska because of the wind. At -30°F, with a 15-mph wind, exposed flesh will freeze within seconds.

I always wear silk or polypropylene underwear under my house clothes. Then when going outdoors in the cold, I will layer with a fleece or similar jacket, then put heavy exterior pants on, which are usually down-filled. I wear fur mukluks and a fur-lined parka as the outer layer. Sometimes I will have a warm hat on under my hood, and of course, warm mittens. Gloves are rarely worn in extreme cold—you must use mittens.

I have never followed strict layering protocol like you read

Fur parkas are hard to beat for outerwear, and for decades, the Helmericks family has adopted the Native ways of dressing for the cold. Whether your outerwear is fur or the newest development in cold-weather clothing, we strongly advise layering.

about so often, because I have always relied on my Eskimo-style fur clothing, which is so superior to any store-bought "white man" cold-weather clothing. A good parka, mittens, and mukluks are usually sufficient for our cold-weather needs, and fortunately I learned as a young woman to sew the fur clothing my family needed. Most recently, I have made our parkas out

Protecting your hands from frostbite can involve layering, too. A light pair of gloves under fur mitts is useful for holding in heat.

of sheep hides, because they are very durable and don't shed like the old caribou hide furs.

It is nearly impossible to keep your face warm enough without the protective circle of a fur ruff on your parka hood. The encircling fur need only stick out a short distance from your face to create a protective air space to keep your face from freezing. I use wolf, fox, or wolverine for the ruffs I make.

We used to wear only fur mukluks, but in more recent years, Jim and I have taken to wearing "bunny boots" (developed by the US military) or other cold-weather boots when operating snowmachines or other outdoor winter equipment. This is due to the wear and tear that can occur to soft, fur boots when used around machinery. However, I still rely on my fur mukluks if I'm going to be outdoors for a long period.

—*Teena Helmericks*

We still wear comfortable mukluks, handmade skin boots, or a winter boot that's been popular in Alaska since World War II: the bunny boot.

3 How to Bake in a Wood-Fired Oven

JOY ORTH, Sergief Island, Southeast Alaska
Alaskan since 1979

Joy was in her fifties when she and Lloyd set out for a new chapter living on an island near the mouth of the Stikine River. *(Photo courtesy Joy Orth)*

During a trip to British Columbia in 1967, Lloyd and Joy Orth decided it was time to take stock. The Washington State couple talked about a move "closer to nature, not so geared toward material possession," as Joy would later write. But it would take years of scouting before they found their Alaska dream: a 114-acre parcel on Sergief Island, where the fresh water of the Stikine River met the Inside Passage, where forested mountains cut into the horizon, and solitude was a certainty.

"I got lonely sometimes," Joy remembers. "Most of the people who came up the river, some would stop, and they were all congenial people. I suppose it gave me a real love of isolation."

In December 1979, the family found themselves in Wrangell, unable to boat the last ten miles to Sergief due to tricky river ice. Finally arriving on March 17, 1980, they began the hard work of living simply. Seven years later, Joy would publish details of their experiences in *Island: Our Alaskan Dream and Reality*.

They wanted to be close to nature, and they got it: repairing buildings, gardening, hunting, fishing, gathering wood and water, dealing with bears, homeschooling their kids . . . and cooking on a wood-fired stove. The Orths had bought their Waterford Stanley stove in 1971 for a whopping $900. The next question was how to get it to the island.

"We hauled it tenderly over the icy winter roads of British Columbia," Joy wrote, "barged it over the troubled waters to Sergief Island, grunted it off the barge, up the bank, and into the cabin."

The nuances of cooking with wood required lots of experimentation, which led to great fodder for her memoir. Like the day daughter Sethnie came running out to the garden, yelling, "Mom, something's coming out of the oven!"

Joy rushed in to find flowing dough had nearly sealed the oven door. She described the loaves as "pale and sagging in the middle," and went about rekindling the fire.

"I set the pitiful mess on the table that night. There was no running to the store for a quick replacement to save my wounded pride."

A decade after landing on the island, Lloyd's serious illness forced the couple to sell their place. Joy was in her sixties, far from ready to "retire." They looked for a town with few people and lots of natural beauty. Their choice back in western Washington fit the bill, she says, but it paled compared to the real thing.

"I don't think anybody who's ever lived out in the wilderness, if they liked it at all, would choose another way if they could," Joy said some twenty years later. "It's a way of life that's hard to beat."

"I wish I was still there," she said nearly thirty-five years later. "I'm older now and I'm having a hard time doing much work, but I'd rather be there than here. Someday I'll go back if I live long enough.

"I haven't made bread since I left Alaska. Kinda sad." ■

The Best Bread

THROUGH TRIAL AND ERROR, I've learned a bit about baking bread. Almost any recipe will do; it's what you do with the recipe that counts. When the book says to knead for eight to ten minutes, it means it. No shortcuts. More kneading after the first rising makes for a lighter, finer-grained loaf, too. Do not allow the loaves to over-rise in the pans.

I start by measuring my hot water into the bowl and go from there. Each cup of water, 1 teaspoon salt, 1 tablespoon sugar or other sweetener, 1 tablespoon shortening will give you about one loaf of bread (depending on the size of the pans) when mixed with sufficient flour (about 4 cups) to make an easily handled dough. Other ingredients are added depending on my fancy. Sometimes all whole-wheat flour,

My Waterford Stanley stove was my treasure, but it took a while for us to make friends. Learning how to feed the fire for a steady heat is a trial-and-error experience.

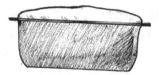

After the first rising, if you punch down the dough for a second kneading, you'll have a finer-grain loaf of bread.

sometimes white, but most often a blend of several different flours or grains.

After being used to continuous heat turned up or down by a dial, it takes a while to learn to remember to check the wood supply in the firebox regularly enough to avoid finding your fire out five minutes after you put the steak in the pan or the cake in the oven. You also must learn the best spot on the range for a particular pan.

Oven temperature is extremely important. When first placing the loaves in the oven, the temperature must be hot enough (around 400°F) to pull the loaves to their maximum size and hold them while a crust is formed with enough strength to give the loaf stability. Once this point is reached, by shutting down the vents, oven temperature may be reduced to around 300°F to complete baking. If the loaves sound hollow when tapped, they're done.

If either of these points is neglected (lengthy kneading or too-low temperature at first), the result will be crumbly, full of holes, or flat.

—Joy Orth

4 How to Start a Chain Saw

KEITH LAUWERS, Anchorage
Alaskan since 1967

Like many Alaskan clergy, Keith Lauwers has probably delivered more wilderness sermons—while fishing, hunting, logging, skiing, or running dogs—than he has from the pulpit. A bearded, barrel-chested man with a demonstrative love for people, Keith has both the build and baritone of Smoky the Bear. When he shakes your hand, you know you've been shaked.

Born in 1936, Keith grew up in British Columbia, where at fourteen, he worked with his father and uncles at his grandfather's logging camp—all of them either logging or trucking or welding.

Keith moved his young family to Alaska in 1967. And while he would return to logging one day, it would be a means to support his ministry, a pattern he followed throughout his career. From that first summer, for twenty-seven seasons, Keith supplemented his pastor's income by commercial fishing, as did many of his flock.

"I was serious at it, but I was never what you'd call a professional, full-time, year-round fisherman. That's what I did for my 'exotic summer cruise.' Mostly in Egegik or Ugashik. And mostly because I had a little church that had more fishermen per capita than any church in Alaska."

In his career as a "tent-maker" pastor, Keith Lauwers fished commercially and developed a logging business to supplement his financial support.
(Photo courtesy Lauwers Family)

For ten years, Keith also led teenaged boys into the mountains of Resurrection Pass for a popular winter Bible camp. The boys skied while Keith mushed dogs, talked about Jesus, and encouraged the kids to follow their dreams.

"I would have the dog team and the freighter sled with the grub, and the sleeping bags, and the cooking utensils," Keith remembers. "And they would have their skis and a little rucksack."

Keith returned to logging when he was pushing sixty, and accepted a post with a parachurch organization to reach Alaska Native communities.

He partnered with two men to form Alaska Mountain Timber, logging and milling spruce beetle–killed trees on the Kenai Peninsula.

"I had a chance to support my ministry either by going around the country to raise support, or to work on my own. I lost some weight and really toughened up. We didn't make any money, but we made some wonderful friends."

For Keith, keeping his chain saw tuned up and sharp was critical to his business. And taking care in starting and handling the equipment was equally important. He jokes about how he used to take some friendly kidding for his start-up method, but he knew that it worked and it was safe—more on that below.

While the logging operation eventually closed, Keith is still a pastor (now emeritus), still an outdoorsman, and still available to friends should a problem tree need cutting. ■

Keeping It Safe

ONE OF THE REAL DANGERS—and I see all kinds of people doing this, but it's very wrong and very dangerous—is to to hold the chain saw in front of you and pull the starting cord. Whenever you jerk it hard, very few have the hand strength in their left hand to just hold the chain saw right in front of them where it's real safe. Almost always that blade will swing a little bit.

What I do, and some guys will make fun of it, I will put the handle of the chain saw between my knees, and then hold it on top, so I've got three stabilizing points—my hand on the top handle, and then between my legs, the other handle—and then when you pull on it, the blade that can really chew up a man's leg in a hurry, it stays right out there.

If it hasn't been started for a while, you want to make sure the choke is pretty well full

It pays to recognize that the chain saw is a tremondous tool. They're a lot lighter and a lot more efficient that they ever used to be, but you just have to respect them.

open, and as you pull on it, if it coughs a time or two, then you can turn the choke down a little bit. Once it gets running, you let it idle so the fuel is really coming well. Before you work it or put a load on the saw, you cut back the choke gradually and give the chain saw a chance to warm up.

The main things are to get your oil and gas mixed properly, to have a sharp chain, so that it cuts straight, and from time to time file down the rakers between the blade of the chain saw. The rakers throw the sawdust out of a cut, and you get maximum cutting power if your teeth

Keeping It Safe (cont'd)

are getting a good bite and the sawdust isn't choking the cut.

You really ought to protect your ears—we didn't do that years ago, and there are hard hats that would protect you in case a limb would fall from above. They even have special chaps that you can put on that really protect your shins in the event that a branch kicks your bar with the blade on. It doesn't have to be going wide open to really tear into you. There's nothing very clean about a chain saw wound.

There was only one time that I took a little slice out of my jeans and just barely touched my kneecap. Well, it grabs your attention.

Most of the time, you can control the direction of a falling tree by how you cut it. The only other factors that would change that is if there was a predominance of heavy branches hanging on one side of the tree, or if there was a strong wind blowing. You don't usually plan to fall a tree into the wind. You arrange to fall it with the wind.

—*Keith Lauwers*

I secure the saw like this, so the blade won't swing when I pull the starting cord.

Use protection for your eyes and ears—and consider buying a pair of logging chaps for bigger jobs. A sharpening tool is essential for maintaining your chain saw, ensuring faster and cleaner cuts.

5 How to Avoid an Avalanche

JILL FREDSTON, Southcentral Alaska
Alaskan since 1982

Choosing Alaska for her adopted state was natural for Jill Fredston, considering she'd earned a master's degree in—as she puts it—"snow and ice." Growing up on a small island north of New York City, Jill had first earned a bachelor's in Physical Geography and Environmental Science from Dartmouth. Later she graduated from Cambridge with a master's in Polar Studies and Glaciology—best used in a state where there's plenty of both geography and glaciers.

"There weren't too many other places I would get a job," Jill says. An opening with the Alaska Avalanche Forecast Center brought the chance to combine her twin loves of science and the outdoors. However, one man who reviewed her resume deemed her unqualified, she said.

"He urged that they hire someone with experience and credibility," Jill remembers. "He was right—I had never even seen an avalanche." Fortunately, Jill landed the job anyway, and in something of a movie twist, she ended up marrying her naysayer, Doug Fesler. For many years, the couple has codirected the Alaska Mountain Safety Center, studying the scientific and subjective aspects of reading the snow, as well as investigating accidents and distributing life-saving information about avalanches.

"I love avalanches," Jill says. "I love the fact that there are so many different combinations of snow layers and that no two avalanches are exactly the same. At the same time, there's a high degree of predictability. I had always learned by swilling facts; avalanches taught me to learn by paying attention and honing my powers of observation."

Few people know that with training, they can improve their survival odds dramatically. With her husband, Jill published a book on evaluating avalanche hazards, led safety workshops, and frequently answered the call when lives were lost.

"There've been more body recoveries than anything else," she says. "I've probably dug over

Jill Fredston's books are aimed at educating backcountry travelers on how to evaluate the risk of avalanche as they're enjoying the outdoors. *(Photo courtesy Jill Fredston)*

forty bodies from avalanche debris and have only helped recover one person alive who was completely buried.

"I will never grow tired of avalanches. I'm pretty tired of the fact that avalanches kill people, and we see the same kind of accidents happening over and over and over again."

For half the year, the avalanche chasers can be found on the water in Alaska's coastal areas, living on a motor-sailor vessel and tooling around by oceangoing rowing boats. And a portion of each year is spent in a home that Jill built in the mountains outside Anchorage.

"I like a place where things are not all figured out," Jill says. "In Alaska, most people didn't blink twice when I started building a house with a fram-

Safety in Snow Country

CHECKLIST QUESTIONS FROM *SNOW SENSE*:

✓ **TERRAIN:** Is it capable of producing an avalanche? Is the slope steep enough to slide? Is it in shadow or sun? What is its shape?

✓ **SNOWPACK:** Could the snow fail? What is the configuration of the slab? How deep? Are there tender spots or a weak layer? How much force would it take to fail or shear?

✓ **WEATHER:** Is it contributing to instability? What type of precipitation, how much, how heavy? Is wind blowing the snow? What's the temperature? Has it stormed or is a storm ahead?

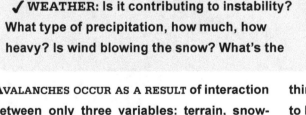

✓ **HUMAN:** What are your alternatives and their possible consequences? What is your attitude to life, toward risk, your goals and assumptions? Are you technically skilled? Do you have the right equipment? Are you strong, prepared for the worst?

AVALANCHES OCCUR AS A RESULT of interaction between only three variables: terrain, snowpack, and weather. But it is a fourth variable—the human factor—that allows most accidents to happen.

Most accidents happen, not because we don't recognize important clues indicating the snow might be unstable, but because we either underestimate the hazard or overestimate our ability to deal with it. We make a lot of decisions based upon what we want or what we think or what we've done before. The reality is that to be safe in the mountains, we need to think like a mountain. Ask yourself, "So what, does the mountain care that it is late or you're tired or you've skied this slope a hundred times before?" The harsh reality is that our assumptions, timetables, needs, skills, and experience make no difference to a hairtrigger snowpack. We have so many filters when we make decisions. The trick is to take the subjectivity out of our decision making.

—*Jill Fredston*

ing book in one hand, or when I'd take off on three- or four-month wilderness trips. I love the wildness that still exists in Alaska, but do I see myself as a pioneer? No. I just like to be able to take care of myself and other people."

Jill has written two books about avalanches in Alaska's mountains: *Snow Sense* in 1999, an instructive book about evaluating hazards; and *Snow Struck* in 2005, a more literary approach to the subject. Jill established herself in the genre of nature writing with her 2002 award-winning book, *Rowing to Latitude*.

We asked for her insights on how to avoid the dangers of an avalanche. ■

INGREDIENTS FOR A SLAB AVALANCHE

SUITABLY STEEP TERRAIN

+

UNSTABLE SNOW STRUCTURE
- **SLAB** *One or more layers; Generally better bonded, more cohesive, and stronger than layer beneath.*
- **WEAK LAYER** *Poorly bonded, weaker grains*
- **BED SURFACE** *Generally stronger than weak layer, sliding surface for slab, can be ground; Other well-bonded, consolidated layers or ground.*

+

CRITICAL BALANCE BETWEEN STRESS/STRENGTH
(i.e. stored elastic energy)

+

SOMETHING TO TIP THE BALANCE
(Likely triggers)

=

AVALANCHE

(Chart used with permission. From *Snow Sense: A Guide to Evaluating Snow Avalanche Hazard*, by Jill A. Fredston and Doug Fesler, Alaska Mountain Safety Center, Inc., Anchorage, Alaska, 1994)

6 How to Build a Snowmachine Sled

CHARLIE LEAN, Nome
Past President, Pioneers of Alaska, Igloo No. 1, Fourth-generation Alaskan

The name Charlie Lean has been around Alaska for more than a century. It started with an English blacksmith named Cleve Lean, nicknamed Charley, who arrived in the early 1900s to help build the Copper River Railroad. In 1910, Charley and his brother Jack were hunting

Charlie with a finished sled in 2003. Constructed to withstand heavy loads and rough terrain, the design was passed down from his father and grandfather, and improved upon with each generation. (Photo courtesy Charlie Lean)

moose on the Kenai Peninsula and decided "Cooper's Landing" looked like a fine place to settle, overlooking the turquoise waters of Kenai Lake. Plenty of trees, plenty of fish and game. In the years that followed, Charley worked as a commercial hunter, providing game meat for towns and railroad construction camps. As for Jack, he contracted with the US government as a dog-team mail carrier and later ran a store.

Charley was thirty-nine in 1919 when he met Beryl, an eighteen-year-old who'd come north from Seattle with her mother and sister to operate a laundry in Seward. When mom wanted out of the laundry business, she decided to marry off her daughters and chose men in their forties. Charley and Beryl set up housekeeping back at Cooper's Landing; Jack remained a lifelong bachelor. The actual "landing" of what's now called Cooper Landing remains in the Lean family. Jack Lean's cabin (and former store and post office) is attached to a museum.

Charley's son, C. N. "Nick" Lean was a self-made man, too, earning two degrees—in mining engineering and mineral engineering—from the Alaska Agricultural College and School of Mines, now known as the University of Alaska Fairbanks. Later on, Nick also earned a professional engineering rating in civil engineering. Nick Lean and family moved all over the territory with each new job, from gold miner to highway engineer.

The current Charlie Lean was born in Fairbanks, and moved to Nome at three months. As his dad changed jobs, they moved back to Fairbanks, on to Douglas, then Fairbanks, then Dillingham. Finally, Charlie settled his own household in Nome, where he works as a fisheries biologist and is well respected for his volunteerism. The governor recognized Charlie with a "Stars of Gold" award for decades of volunteer work as an EMT, as well as service in Rotary Club and Pioneers of Alaska. As a former president of the Pioneers Igloo No. 1, he has a strong appreciation for the old-timers' stories and helps to record them for the archives.

Much of Charlie's practical knowledge of getting along in the North came from his father, such as building sleds—not racing dogsleds, but heavy-duty sleds for moving freight behind a dog team or snowmachine (as snowmobiles are called in Alaska). Given a choice, Charlie says, his father preferred running "iron dogs" to the real thing.

"Dad prospected in the Brooks Range just after World War II," Charlie said. "He had experience with dogs. To put it in his words, 'I'd rather wash dishes than mush dogs.'"

Today, it's far more common to see snowmachines than dogs in Nome, Charlie says; although, he and his wife, Mikey, had a dog team for about a dozen years. Mikey actually entered a few races. But no more dogs now. Charlie jokes that he wasn't built for speed in the first place.

"I'm a big guy—six-five, two fifty—I'm not the jockey."

When snowmachines first arrived in Nome around 1960, they were "pretty strange and not very efficient," Charlie says. "Somewhere about

Charlie Lean's grandfather, Cleve "Charley" Lean, poses with bearskins that he planned to sell as touring-car lap robes, ca. 1915. *(Photo courtesy Charlie Lean)*

1962 or thereabouts, is when snowmachines seriously displaced dogs. I was a small boy, and I'd just moved from Nome to Fairbanks when that happened. There were many loose dogs. A lot of people just turned their dogs loose. Remember, they were livestock, not pets—a very different mind-set then about dogs."

Yet the skills he learned from his dad have been useful for making freight sleds for snowmachine travel.

"The principles are the same, they're just a little bit beefier, more rigid," he says. "Rigid sleds are not able to be steered. Limber sleds steer well, so a used sled and a lighter sled are desirable behind dogs. We use snowmachine sleds for transporting hunting supplies, camping, fuel, and containers. Lots of us go out crabbing on the ice, so crab pots, boards, and tools to do that. An assortment of freight.

"Sleds are frequently loaded with 500 pounds and often as much as 1,000, particularly if hunting is good. A 500-pound load would require about ten modern dogs. In my dad's day, 1959, dogs were larger. Dogs weighed closer to 70 pounds on average."

Charlie has built many sleds over the years, gradually improving his skill in using steam to bend wood and in refining the joints. One of the first sleds he built was in junior high, when the Leans were living in Southeast, and he was a member of Boy Scouts. The big project: every troop had to build its own sled from scratch and tow it.

"We really got into it, my troop in Douglas, and my father remembered building dogsleds as a child with his father, so we built some really quick-and-dirty sleds for the contest. Dad was a little frustrated with that, thought that he could do much better. So my brother, Dad, and I built a fairly good sled out of hardwood, flooring maple actually; it was what we had.

"Dad showed me how to steam and bend wood, how he did it as a child. He showed me how to make rawhide, and we made the sled. It was a beefy sled . . . it was overbuilt."

About ten years later, Charlie and his brother sold that sled to one of the earliest Iditarod Trail Sled Dog Race mushers, who used it to train for the thousand-mile race. Back, full circle, to the dogs. ■

Charlie Lean and Tom Vaden work on fastening the skid strips to the bottom of the freight sled. If the sled rides over small brush, freight on the top deck will be protected by the strips. *(Photo courtesy Charlie Lean)*

An Old-Style Sled

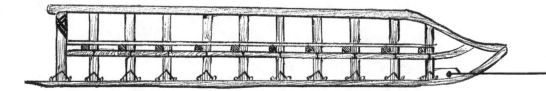

I'VE BUILT SO MANY SLEDS, they rarely look the same. I do try to improve. I look for ideas, so as a consequence my sleds morph over time, and I'm not stuck in one mold. Right around the 1980s, I started to build sleds in a serious way, and I read some books on wood bending and improved my bending technique a lot.

This sled is 42 inches across and 10 feet long. In this case I had thirteen slats forming the deck and six forming a skid plate. The skid plate is important if you straddle a stump or rock. The skid strips cover the cracks of the floor slats so brush does not whip the load from underneath.

This sled is too wide to ride the runners—it's for towing, usually behind a snowmachine. The rails are straight, parallel to the ground. No handlebar; they end at the end of the runner. The runners terminate about 4 inches beyond the last stanchion. This is so you can carry a boat or large item on the rails with even support.

You begin with 2-by-8-by-12 "green" or "bending" hickory planks, relatively clear of knots. As you cut slats, cross members, and vertical stanchions, cut around any knots. The runners and top rail must be steam bent. First you soak the wood until it's saturated, up to two weeks. To steam it, I use a camp stove, a can for boiling the water, and some stovepipe. Put multiple pieces of wood in the horizontal stovepipe and cork it with insulation to keep the steam in. Add water to the can—do not let it boil dry. I use a meat thermometer and keep the temperature in the pipe between 210° and 212°F for ½ hour for every ¼ inch of thickness.

There are six stanchions on either side of the sled. The cross members are bolted to the two rails that are on either side of the stanchions. The top rail is 7 inches above the deck. To hold the top rail to the top of the stanchions, I used a strap of UHMW (¼ inch thick) held in place with a ¼ inch-diameter bolt.

The stanchions have mortise-and-tenon joints to the runner. I've found over time, you try to avoid corners in the mortise holes, so now we drill a hole and then create an oval tenon peg, as opposed to a square or rectan-

An Old-Style Sled (cont'd)

TO STEAM

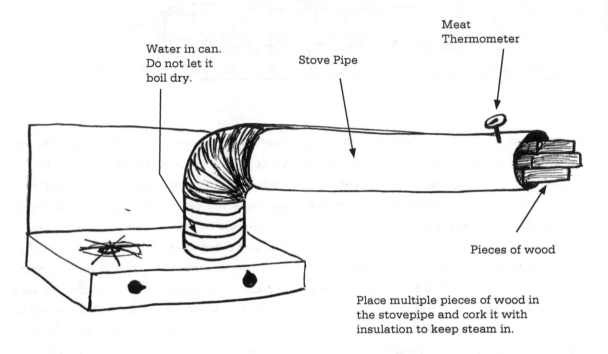

Water in can. Do not let it boil dry.

Stove Pipe

Meat Thermometer

Pieces of wood

Place multiple pieces of wood in the stovepipe and cork it with insulation to keep steam in.

gular tenon peg. If you put sharp corners in the wrong place, it'll just split out. Also, at each intersection with the cross member and the slat, use only one screw (#12 x 1½-inch Phillips). Use more and it will split when it flexes.

The runners are composed of 3½-inch thick layers (laminations). The mortise hole only penetrates the top lamination. The mortise-and-tenon joints are lashed in using eye bolts about 2 inches fore and aft of the stan-chion post and holes through the stanchion about 3 inches above the runner. I use 120# test tuna leader for lashing. The eye bolts penetrate the entire depth of the runner and are counter sunk on the bottom side and cut flush so the plastic wear strip fits well. I often set washers on either side of the runner on the shank off the eye bolt so they do not wear out the wood.

The front cross member is very heavy to withstand impact. I use ⁵⁄₁₆-inch or larger car-

ATTACH TO SLED WITH:

- Angle iron, at least ¼" thick
- Lock nuts
- Lag bolts going to the runners, ⁵⁄₁₆" and 1½" long

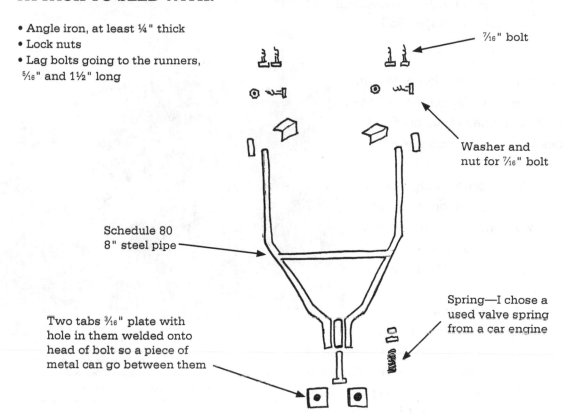

⁷⁄₁₆" bolt

Washer and nut for ⁷⁄₁₆" bolt

Schedule 80 8" steel pipe

Two tabs ³⁄₁₆" plate with hole in them welded onto head of bolt so a piece of metal can go between them

Spring—I chose a used valve spring from a car engine

riage bolts to fasten the runners, rails, and slats to this piece.

To protect the runners, attach a 4-inch-wide strip of UHMW recycled plastic along the 10 foot length of the runners. The plastic is wide to help ride on the snow. To that I center another narrower strip, measuring 2 inches by ¾ inch, that comes in contact with the ground. That's a wear strip that's easily replaced. The towing yolk is attached to the runners with

¼-inch angle iron and lag bolts ⁵⁄₁₆ inch by 1½ inches long.

This is all just what I did in this case. Of the fifty or so wood sleds I have built, no three are exactly the same. Only twice I built identical pairs.

—Charlie Lean

7 How to Field Dress a Moose

JOEL DONER, Anchorage and Clam Gulch
Alaskan since 1968

Joel Doner hails from a family of commercial set-net fishermen whose patriarch homesteaded at Anchor Point in 1950, back before there was a road linking them with the rest of the state. At the homestead, Joel's father Doug finished high school by correspondence and grew up on the Kenai Peninsula staples of "moose and potatoes, moose and potatoes, moose and potatoes," as he used to joke.

Doug went to college in southern California, married, and started a family. But he remained homesick for the freedom and opportunities of the Last Frontier. So in the summer of 1968, the Doners moved back. After a summer of fishing Cook Inlet, Doug got an offer from the Anchorage School District, and just in time.

"We were staying in Russian Jack Springs Park—the whole family and a dog . . . with puppies!" Joel remembers. "We were basically homeless in Russian Jack when my dad found a job. Five kids—pretty young, too. We had a van, and my parents slept in the van and then us five kids in that travel trailer. And the puppies."

From that day onward, the rhythms of the year were based on teaching school in winters, and commercial fishing in summers at Clam Gulch. For decades, Joel's parents, siblings, their spouses, and kids all worked and played their summers

Joel bagged this magnificent bull moose several years ago. Every backcountry hunter knows that once the adrenaline fades, you're faced with packing out hundreds of pounds of meat. *(Photo courtesy Joel Doner)*

away at the Alaskan version of a beach, hauling fish into their skiffs during short, intense openers; building campfires; paddling in the surf; and running free. Summers with lots of salmon; summers with few salmon. The tradition continued after Doug's death in 1997, and the multifamily Doner commercial fishing sites remain a gathering place each summer. Now a fourth generation is grown and taking over one of the state-regulated permit sites while home from college.

As for Joel, when he was a hard-driving single man, he also worked the highly competitive salmon openers of Bristol Bay, and spent weeks away from town. Now married and a father of two, Joel earns a living fishing the Cook Inlet setnet site, running a snowplow business, and working as a big-game guide for bear, Dall sheep, and moose.

The Alaska Department of Fish and Game says tens of thousands of Alaskans, urban and rural, hunt for moose each fall, taking more than 7,000 animals from a statewide population of about 175,000. Along with nonresident hunters, the total comes to about 3.5 million pounds of meat a year. State law requires that, whether you're a trophy hunter or a meat hunter, all moose and caribou meat must be salvaged for human consumption. It is legal to leave the head, skin, organs, and bones in the field.

"When you kill a Dall sheep, you get sixty pounds of meat," Joel says. "When you kill a moose, you've got hundreds of pounds . . . but then you have to pack it out."

During two decades of guiding hunters, Joel has learned the most important principle is to immediately get to work on cooling the meat, so he offered these instructions on how to field dress a moose. ■

Working in the Field

THE INSTANT A MOOSE DIES, the meat starts going bad. The main purpose of skinning it is to get the meat cool. The only way to do that is to cut it up into chunks and get it up off the ground to cool, and get the skin off of it.

Moose die where they're standing, and they're notorious for being in the swamps. You've got a handful then. I've just never been lucky enough to have equipment when it happens. You just grab on, get it as close to shore as possible, and start cutting. It's not very precise stuff. Just get chunks that you can handle.

I've never skinned a moose exactly the same way, because they're always laying in a different place. They're never laying in the same hole, in the same position. Sometimes I'm only concerned about the meat; other times I'm guiding, and then it's the trophy I'm thinking about.

Must-have Tools for Field Dressing a Moose

1. At least one sharp skinning knife
2. Knife sharpener
3. 100-foot rope or line
4. Poly tarp (for setting clean meat on and covering meat)
5. Game bags
6. Bone/brush saw or hatchet
7. Heavy-duty backpack with heavy-duty back attached
8. Survey flagging to find kill site

Working in the Field (cont'd)

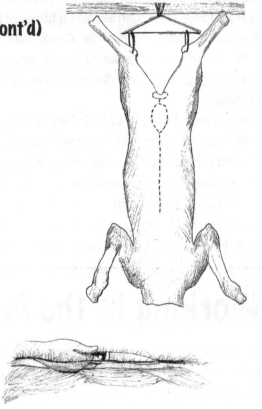

You've got to know where those joints are. You cannot carry the back half of a moose. You can barely roll it around. You're lucky to get just one of the parts off because it might be in a hole or something.

On the tundra, there are leaves and sticks everywhere, so keeping the meat clean is very important. And keeping hair off of it.

In a perfect world, if the moose is hanging up, I want to peel the skin off from the belly around the back. You can flop the skin down [hair-side down], and start putting meat on the skin to keep it clean. Using a game bag or wrap keeps bugs off, keeps it clean, and makes handling and hanging it easier. You can buy a game bag, and a lot of them come with instructions.

—*Joel Doner*

Skinning is easier if the animal is hanging, but if that's not possible, you must dress it where it falls. Begin at the belly and keep the cut shallow—do not plunge the blade straight into the belly or you'll pierce the organs. Once the skin is removed, lay it out on the ground, fur-side down, and lay chunks of meat on it as you work.

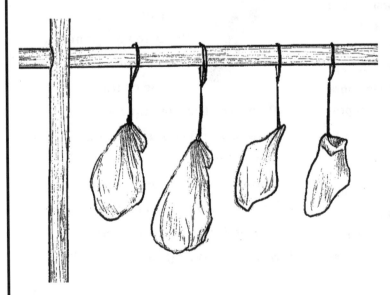

After the meat is cooled and dry, use commercially made game bags to keep it clean and insect-free. Old-timers used pepper on field-dressed meat to keep bugs off. Available today is a high-acid spray to prevent bacterial or insect contamination.

8 How to Take Care of Your Sourdough

LISA FREDERIC, Uganik Island and Denali Park
Alaskan since 1981

Lisa Frederic is fascinated by the histories of various sourdough starters. She discovered some true Alaskan characters as she traced the "genealogy" of her Golden Spoon starter. *(Photo courtesy Lisa Frederic)*

Lisa Frederic was a twenty-one-year-old horsewoman from Kentucky when she landed in Kodiak in 1981. She found a cannery job and joined other workers in an illegal tent encampment at the edge of town. It rained, she later wrote, "almost constantly, not gently or softly, but in a roar and with great force." Nevertheless, Lisa immediately knew she'd spend the rest of her life here.

Lisa would live out her childhood fantasy: herding cattle on a Kodiak ranch, working as a halibut boat deckhand, finding love and home with a man named David Little. In 1985, Lisa and David bought a commercial salmon permit, and for decades they fished together and lived in a remote cabin on Uganik, one of many islands in the Kodiak Archipelago.

You'd think that would be adventure enough for one lifetime. But in 1997, Lisa was watching the end of the Iditarod Trail Sled Dog Race in Nome, and was stirred by the relationship between mushers and sled dogs. Five years later, she found herself at the starting line of the thousand-mile race—middle-aged, anxious, but ready to run a team of young dogs for her boss, Iditarod champion Jeff King. She later wrote about the hard work and hysterics of her experience in *Running with Champions*.

But wait, there's more. Lisa—still fishing, still working with dogs—next discovered a fascination with sourdough, that amazing, living substance that was carried North with the gold rush stampeders. Sourdough was so common that old-timers themselves became known as "Sourdoughs."

"Everyone loves it because it's such a cheap food," says Lisa, also citing its portability and how it's almost magically reconstituted from its dormant state. "One of my neighbors in Uganik, another woman who was fishing, had forgotten to bring her sourdough out. But she had her spoon that she always used with her. It was clean, but there were enough microbes on it that she was able to reconstitute it!"

Lisa's latest joy is tracking sourdough "lines," which are especially treasured when provenance can be shown. She's built a small business of packaging and selling wooden spoons coated in a starter given to her by fellow musher Dean Osmar. It can be traced back to 1944 and pioneer Alaskans Babe and Mary Alsworth of Lake Clark. Lisa calls her product "Alaska's Golden Spoon" and makes it available online at www.alaskasgoldenspoon.com.

Online sources tell how to start sourdough in various ways. Following are Lisa's tips for starting from her spoons, and keeping it alive for years to come. ■

Lisa draws stories from her years in commercial fishing and dog mushing to share with tourists to Denali National Park & Preserve. She currently spends her summers driving busloads of visitors into the national park. (Photo courtesy Lisa Frederic)

SOAK THE COATED PORTION of the Golden Spoon in ½ cup warm water. (Not too hot—it could kill the yeast! Test the water on your wrist like a baby's bottle.) A small jelly jar works real well. The dried sourdough starter will turn the water cloudy after a half hour or so, then you can blend in ¾ cup white flour. The mixture should have a consistency of a thick pancake mix. Add more warm water if you need to. Lightly cover the container and set it somewhere warm—80°F is an ideal temperature.

Over the next two days occasionally stir your starter using a wooden or plastic spoon, and you will start seeing tiny bubbles appear as the sourdough starts "working." After a couple of days you will see that the mixture is full of bubbles and has almost doubled in size. Add another cup of flour and enough warm water to make a consistency once again similar to a thick pancake mix. Let this "work" for another twelve hours or so.

You can now use the starter following any sourdough recipe! Just remember to save a small amount of pure starter. Even a tablespoonful will get you going. Personally I keep a small sour-

Baking Like a Sourdough

Sourdough bread and pancakes are just the start. After removing a portion of your starter for baking, replenish the mixture by adding equal parts of water and flour, stir, and return to the refrigerator. You'll have plenty for many more of your favorite recipes.

dough pot in the refrigerator. When I am interested in using some, I pull out the jar to let it warm up to room temperature overnight. I pull out a cup or so of starter—depending on the recipe—and put it in a bowl with the specific amount of flour called for.

When you use some starter from your sourdough pot, replenish it by adding a cup or so of the flour-and-water mixture that's the consistency of thick pancake mix. As long as you save at least a tablespoon of pure starter, you can rebuild the amount of sourdough in your pot by feeding it. Always keep the starter pure—nothing but flour and water goes into the pot!

—*Lisa Frederic*

Sourdough Banana Bread

½ cup shortening
1 cup granulated sugar
1 large egg
1 cup mashed bananas
1 cup active sourdough starter
1 teaspoon vanilla extract or
   1 teaspoon grated orange peel
2 cups unbleached flour
1 teaspoon salt
1 teaspoon baking powder
½ teaspoon baking soda
¾ cup chopped walnuts

Cream together the shortening and sugar, add egg, and mix until blended. Stir in bananas and sourdough starter. Add vanilla or orange peel. Stir flour and measure again with salt, baking powder, and soda. Add flour mixture and walnuts to the first mixture, stirring until just blended. Pour into greased 9-by-5-inch loaf pan. Bake in 350°F oven for 1 hour or until wooden pick comes out clean. Cool.

9 How to Build a Dock

RAY WILLIAMS, Pile Bay and Anchor Point
Alaskan since 1951

Ray Williams is a truck driver, true, but don't get him confused with the typical truckers of the Lower 48 road system. His "highway" is just fifteen miles long, an unpaved roadway wending between an unpopulated dot on Cook Inlet called Williamsport, over the rocky Chigmit Mountains, to a barely populated dot on Lake Iliamna called Pile Bay. This really short-haul trucker does business on the only land link between two great bodies of water, delivering essentials to the people of the Bristol Bay region. And while it's a state road, nestled on each end is Williams land that has been in the family for three generations.

Above: Ray and Linda were grade-school sweethearts who eventually married and grew the Williams family business in remote Pile Bay. Now an adult, their son Chet, right, is the third generation to work along this fifteen-mile Bush "highway."

Above Right: Iliamna Transportation is the name of the Williams family business that hauls, among other freight, commercial fishing boats.
(Photos courtesy Ray Williams)

In winters, the Pile Bay-Williamsport Road is under about five or six feet of snow, and Ray and family spend the months in the little town of Anchor Point, on the Kenai Peninsula. But the summers are hopping with freight, boats, and people steadily arriving at Williamsport for passage over the road to Pile Bay, a tide that reverses before the snow flies.

Perhaps Ray's most unusual cargo are commercial fishing boats heading for the world-fam-ous fishing grounds of Bristol Bay. From various home ports, they navigate Cook Inlet to Williamsport for portage over the road to the 1,000-square-mile Lake Iliamna, the eighth-largest lake in the nation. Entering Lake Iliamna at Pile Bay, the boats travel south to the Kvichak River, a deep and broad stream that flows sixty more miles before entering Bristol Bay. Captains who use the portage can shave off hundreds of miles—and many gallons of diesel—by not rounding the Alaska Peninsula. Save time and money? Hard to beat that combination. Still, Ray won't take vessels wider than fourteen feet—a safety limitation, he says.

"There are a couple places on the mountain where the bluff is just too close."

The freight-hauling business has been in the Williams family since Ray's pioneer father, Carl, bought the property, with a horse and truck, in 1935. A couple years later, Ray's parents set up housekeeping at "Williamsport," as they called their place. Back then, the mail came twice a year by barge, and motorized vessels were as yet illegal in Bristol Bay.

The road followed an ancient route that was used by Alaska Natives and later, Russian travelers. It was mapped by the US Geological Survey as early as 1909. Carl partnered with his brother, Lyle, and made road improvements, then in 1937 the brothers extended the route to Pile Bay. With one brother at each end of the fifteen road-miles, the Williams men had a smooth operation, until tragedy struck. In 1944, Lyle was killed in an accident along the road, at a place now known as "Lyle's Bend." He was buried nearby.

One year the family moved to Pile Bay so the kids could join a handful of other children who were schooled there. Later still, they spent their winters on the Kenai Peninsula, so Ray's older siblings could attend high school. Over four decades, the buildings at Williamsport have come to ruin in the mean weather—fallen buildings, household debris, and a rusting old truck. Meanwhile, the Pile Bay property improved.

The width of the vessel determines if it can be moved over the highway, limited by the width of bridges that span several streams on the route.
(Photos courtesy Ray Williams)

In 1972, Ray married Linda, his grade-school sweetheart, and together they built a beautifully appointed, 3,000-square-foot custom home on the northeast tip of Lake Iliamna. The outbuildings at Pile Bay have expanded through the years to include guest cabins, a powerhouse, meat cache, lumberyard, and others. Anchorage is only about 200 air miles away, but standing on the shore of Lake Iliamna, you could swear you were at the edge of the earth. The family spends their summers here, eating game meat, growing their own vegetables, baking bread, keeping chickens, and welcoming guests.

In the Williams family's seventieth year of business, they hauled a record seventy-four commercial fishing boats on the Pile Bay–Williamsport Road. And Ray and Linda's grown son holds an essential role in the operation, ensuring that there'll be a Williams on this road for many years to come. ■

MY DAD USED THIS METHOD and a lot of the Native people around the lakes here used them for years.

In spring on the lake, you still want at least 1½ to 2 feet of water [to build in]. But you've got to be ready for the lake to raise 5 feet.

A lake dock sometimes will have two or three units made up of logs making about an 8-foot square. You stack logs (6- to 8-inch diameter) and spike the corners all the way through to make a crib. Usually just one crib, but I've seen two or three put together to make a longer dock.

You build a big crib until it gets to the height that you want, and then fill it at least half

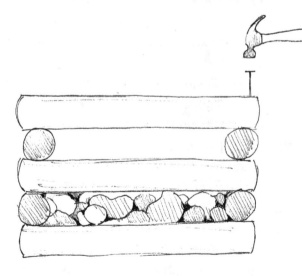

Spike the corners to join the stacked logs that will serve as supports for the dock. Fill the log cribs about halfway up with big rocks.

A Plan That's Simple and Strong

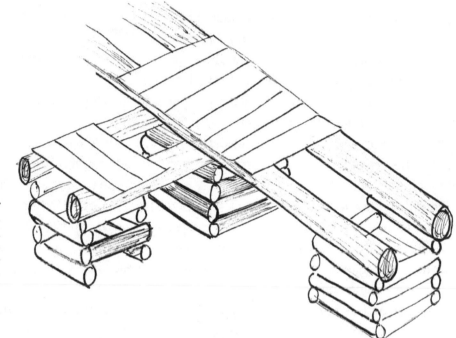

In spring, our water is shallow enough that we can build these in place. The crib supports are joined by log poles; nail deck boards (or use more poles) on top.

full with big rocks to help hold it in place.

Once all of that is put together, take a couple more logs to join the cribs together and then just deck them all over to make your main walkway. Originally, in the old days, they were decked with small poles, 2- to 3-inch diameter poles, until lumber came around.

Usually they last several years. The two things that seem to affect them, is number one, they have a tendency to rot out, of course, and the ice has a tendency to beat it up a bit, espe-cially if the ice can start moving and build up momentum.

There's docks I've seen when I was a kid that were there for years and years and years; then they'd build a new one in a different place and that would only last one or two years, be-cause of where it was. You get even a small amount of ice that's moving . . .

On moving water, like a river, you'd have one bulkhead outside off the riverbank a ways, and a walkway back in.

—*Ray Williams*

10 How to Cross a River Safely

SHERRY SIMPSON, Juneau, Petersburg, Fairbanks, Anchorage
Alaskan since 1967

Solo treks necessitate self-portraits. Here's Sherry's from one trip into Wrangell-St. Elias National Park. *(Photo courtesy Sherry Simpson)*

All the best adventure books are about boys. That's how it seemed to Sherry Simpson when she was growing up in Juneau. So when Sherry's great-aunt gave her a book of blank pages, she filled them with a survival story of her own making, starring a girl, of course.

"When I was a kid, I loved being out in the woods," she remembers. "I was the weirdo who had moccasins and a fort."

Four decades later, Sherry's still exploring the woods and writing about her adventures when she's not teaching in the university system. And she's traded her moccasins for XtraTufs®, her preferred hiking boot.

Sherry was newly inspired to get out in the backcountry during the mid-1990s, while researching historic trails for the state. She'd already earned a bachelor's in journalism, had worked in television and newspapers in Fairbanks and Juneau, then returned to college for a master of fine arts in creative writing. In the archives, she studied old Alaska maps crisscrossed with thin lines—trails to forgotten places. Men carried the US mail by dog team on those trails. In gold country, cities sprouted and died within a few years. Polar explorers pressed the edges of what was then known.

"I'd always liked history and the old-time stories about what people did," Sherry says. "I got interested in why people did those kinds of expeditions, and was it even possible to discover any-thing when you're a middle-aged woman . . . My original ideal was to retrace some of those historic expeditions."

Since then, Sherry's forays—hiking, rafting, camping, and flying—have led her into some of Alaska's most remote places. She's written two collections of essays, countless newspaper articles, contributions to literary anthologies, reviews, and dozens of columns, all with her trademark conversational approach instilled with laserlike insight and a skosh of self-deprecating humor. Often she joins scientists in the field, learning as she goes and asking the questions you'd ask if you could. Where there's controversy, she is a voice of reason and mercy and wonder. Like wolf trapping. Good or bad? Or bears in the city, killed because they're in the wrong place at the wrong time. Or standing in a gold-rush ghost town after days of hiking and wondering about social life and commerce here a century ago.

"I think it's almost impossible to not have preconceived ideas," Sherry says. "I'm interested in discovering what I don't know. In the process of writing—like the wolf trapping—I discover what I do think about it, or thought I did." ■

Ultimate Buddy System

Scout the banks of the river; don't try to cross at a cut-bank (since you don't usually have a choice of which side of the river you're on). If it's a glacial river that's silty, you can't always see the bottom, so you have to be extra careful. That's a good time to have a walking stick to probe.

Listen to the river: if you hear rocks moving, that means the current's really strong. If you can find part of the river that's braided, it'll be shallower. All the power won't be in one course of it.

Before you get in the river, make sure that your backpack's shoulder straps are loose and that the hip buckle is undone, cause if you fall, you want to get out of it quickly.

Tie everything securely so you don't lose your sleeping bag or your bear spray . . . Store your clothes and sleeping bag in really thick plastic bags—trash compactor bags are better than garbage bags—so you have a fighting chance to keep things dry.

Footwear: a lot of people take their boots off; they'll cross in hiking sandals. I wouldn't recommend going in your bare feet. I've known people who've hit a rock and lost toenails and not known it because it's so cold.

It's hard for my feet to warm up. I learned that if your wear neoprene socks inside XtraTufs® and cross, your boots might fill with water, but it's like a scuba suit: it's soft and you warm up.

If you cross with people in a group, it can be really helpful to either go in a chain, holding onto each other's packs, the tallest person first, or link arms. If the water reaches a certain place on the tallest person's thighs, it would be waist deep for someone else, and that's just too deep.

Cross at an angle. Some people think you should angle downstream, so you're not fighting the current. But sometimes you can brace yourself better going upstream. Look ahead. Don't stare down at the water. It's really easy to get dizzy. Kind of shuffle your feet along the bottom.

Don't be afraid to turn back. If someone's not comfortable, they should not feel bad about saying, "Can we go back and try somewhere else?" I've been that person. It's hard sometimes because other people get annoyed, but trying to pull someone out of the water with everything wet is a lot more trouble than going back.

—*Sherry Simpson*

11 How to Live Among Bears

ROY CORRAL, Fairbanks, Brooks Range, Southcentral
Alaskan since 1964

Roy's love for Alaska's wilderness, its people and animals, inspire his writing and photography. *(Photo by Ben Corral)*

As a boy growing up in the Philippines, Roy Corral tromped through the jungle and dreamed of becoming a mountain man. So when the military transferred his family to Fairbanks, Alaska, teenaged Roy thought he'd gone to heaven.

"I continued to go deeper into the woods," he remembers. "I always kinda wanted to find a place of my own."

Into his twenties, Roy pursued his dream with deliberation, researching homesteading laws, studying maps, and working to pay for air charters to remote sites. Then he read a life-changing book: *One Man's Wilderness*, by Dick Proenneke, a skilled craftsman and outdoorsman who kept detailed journals and films while building his Alaska cabin, hunting for food, observing the wildlife, and recording seasonal changes in his world.

"It was my bible," Roy remembers. *One Man's Wilderness* was one of three books that Roy brought along in the early 1970s, when he finally staked his own forty-acre homestead in the Brooks Range at a site he describes as "the edge of the boreal forest, where the forest stopped and the North Slope started." The other two books concerned how to build a cabin. Beyond building a doghouse, Roy had zero experience in carpentry. At last, he was living in solitude.

"This place was perfect for me because people couldn't get up there," he remembers.

In no time, Roy found out why. The area was called Bear Valley for good reason. Both blacks and grizzlies inhabited the area, and they were plentiful.

Building a cabin in the Brooks Range was a feat for a young man who'd built little more than a doghouse before then. *(Photo courtesy Roy Corral)*

"Every day I could always count on seeing three, four bears," he remembers.

Roy's "neighbors" watched, skirting the property as he cut trees and built the cabin. He followed the basics of handling and storing food in bear country, and kept a pile of rocks by the door—along with his rifle, just in case. Rock-throwing kept some bears away. When another poked its nose into the cabin, Roy grabbed the closest "weapon"—a broom—and banged it on the head. Yet another required a round over its head into the trees, sending it running.

"I believe that bears do have a reason for doing the things that they do," he says, "and it's just because of our lack of understanding that their behavior seems unpredictable. They'll give you lots of signals. I've never had to kill a bear in defense of life or property, and I'm pretty proud of that."

Periodically, when it was time to earn more money, Roy buttoned up the cabin against almost certain intrusion. He stored some goods in his cache, some under the cabin, and he barricaded the windows and door with nail-studded plywood. But his bear-proofing, as it turns out, was cub's play.

"What I learned about the plywood is that you had to make it flush with the doorjamb, so the bears can't get their claws underneath," he says. "When I got in there, it looked like a bomb went off. Outside the cabin was just littered with paper. I had a library of books up there and they tore all that stuff up." Roy well remembers picking up the confetti—of one book, in particular.

"I do know that *One Man's Wilderness* was digested," he laughs. "I found pages of it over here and over there . . . "

Roy discovered if keeping them out doesn't work, it's best to just empty the place and leave the door open wide. Afterward, that's just what he did.

Roy said farewell to his homestead in 1984, but the lessons from the Brooks Range have stayed with him for life.

"Part of me grew up there, spiritually and every which way. I matured up there—under-

The cabin was in an ideal place, unless you minded the company of bears.
(*Photo courtesy Roy Corral*)

standing about my relationship with the land and the animals and my place on the planet."

Roy "grew up" to become a writer and photographer. His images of Alaska's wildlife and people have appeared in numerous magazines and books, and Roy's greatest pleasures still lie in tromping around Alaska's backcountry. ■

This Ain't No Theme Park

I WAS CERTAINLY ONE OF THOSE who got sucked into believing that the only defense in bear country was a large-caliber rifle or pistol. I carried both, and suffered from "bearanoia" and insomnia in the wilderness until I began to educate myself about bear behavior.

Today people are accessing Alaska's wilderness armed with much more effective tools than a firearm, including more effective bear sprays, and more importantly, having the knowledge of how to travel safely and what to do in case of a bear encounter. I recommend a close study of the Alaska Department of Fish and Game (ADF&G) website for that. Look for it at www.adf&g.state.ak.us.

If you have handled your food and garbage correctly and still have to kill a bear (to defend your life or property), shoot to kill. Again, check with ADF&G for the legal follow-up steps of handling such a situation. Read up ahead of time and you should be fine.

Some practical advice on living among bears from the Alaska Department of Fish & Game:

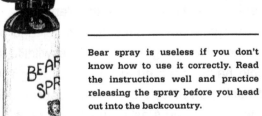

Bear spray is useless if you don't know how to use it correctly. Read the instructions well and practice releasing the spray before you head out into the backcountry.

IN CASE OF A PROBLEM:

- Stay in a safe spot, indoors or in a vehicle, or stand close together with three or more people.
- Make noise to scare the bear. Yell, bang pans, etc.
- If the bear is not threatening, watch it and try to figure out why it is attracted to your home or camp. Fix the problem after the bear leaves. You can call your local Fish and Game office for suggestions.
- If the bear is threatening a person's life or your property, call 911, the local Fish and Game office, and/or shoot the bear yourself.
- Remember, if the bear has been attracted to your home or camp by improperly stored food or garbage, it can NOT be legally killed.

FOOD AND GARBAGE STORAGE:

- Store food and/or garbage in heavier gauge steel barrels with locking lids. Another option for bear-resistant storage is a heavy-gauge aluminum box and pannier.

- The US Forest Service criteria for bear-proof containers include: "(a) resist a direct force of 200 pounds; and (b) contain no cracks, external hinges, gaps, etc., by

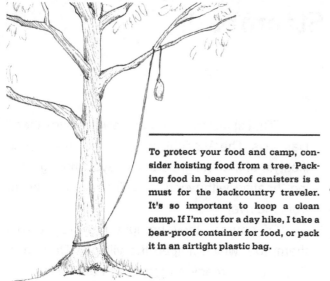

To protect your food and camp, consider hoisting food from a tree. Packing food in bear-proof canisters is a must for the backcountry traveler. It's so important to keep a clean camp. If I'm out for a day hike, I take a bear-proof container for food, or pack it in an airtight plastic bag.

which a bear can force the container open using claws or teeth."

- The Alaska Department of Fish & Game Division of Wildlife Conservation recommends incinerating garbage, not just burning it in a barrel or pit, which can work just the opposite and attract bears.

- You may kill a bear in defense of your life

For both food and garbage, the general rule is, "Pack it in, pack it out." You can also use the bear-proof container for your waste. When you're out camping for extended periods of time, burning is best. I burned my garbage at the Brooks Range homestead. You have to be careful that it's completely incinerated, otherwise it can actually attract bears. For larger camps, store food in specially made heavy-gauge aluminum boxes or barrels with locking lids. Use commercially made incinerators.

or property if you did not provoke an attack or cause a problem by negligently leaving human or pet food or garbage in a manner that attracts bears and if you have done everything else you can to protect your life and property. If you have to shoot, shoot to kill.

- Property means your dwelling, means of travel, pets or livestock, fish drying racks, or other valuable property necessary for your livelihood or survival.

- While game meat is considered your property, you may not kill a bear to protect it unless the meat is critical for your survival. Even in this situation you still must do everything possible to protect the meat (i.e. proper storage, scaring the scavenger, etc.) before you may kill the bear.

Bears killed in defense of life or property belong to the state. If you kill a bear you must remove the hide. If it is a brown bear you must also salvage the skull. You must give both the hide, with claws attached, and the skull to ADF&G. You must also notify your local ADF&G Wildlife Conservation office or Alaska State Troopers Bureau of Wildlife Enforcement immediately. You are required to fill out and submit a questionnaire concerning the circumstances within fifteen days.

—Roy Corral

12 How to Build a Steambath
DAN AUSDAHL, Kuskokwim River
Alaskan since 1958

Dan Ausdahl has spent most of his life in a tiny village on a bend of the Kuskokwim River, accessible only by water or air. Dan's Norwegian heritage conferred him with blond hair, blue eyes, and ruddy cheeks. But growing up among Native Alaskans, marrying a Yup'ik woman, and raising five kids, Dan's lifestyle is more in step with ancient Alaskans than Norwegians. Or perhaps not, where steambaths are concerned.

Born in Minnesota in 1954, Dan was just four when his family moved to Seward. His missionary father took them further out to southwestern Alaska in 1960, and they settled in a Yup'ik village of fewer than 150 people. Their first home was a cabin measuring fourteen-by-sixteen for a family that would grow to seven children.

"[That's] just the way cabins were back then," Dan says. The Ausdahls adopted the subsistence lifestyle of their neighbors, he says, hunting, fishing, heating with wood, and drawing their water from the river.

"Of course, they brought new ideas with them, too, which helped the village," Dan says. "Mom was already a registered nurse, so in the medical field she helped out a lot. Dad, he knew a lot of gardening and stuff, so it was helpful to the community back then. Fresh ideas. Makes life easier.

"There's a lot you can do out here where people think you're on an ice field or something, but that's not the case."

In 2007, Dan helped his sister and brother-in-law build their own steambath outside their Anchorage home. *(Photo courtesy Becky and Renee Contreras)*

Dan's father, Martin, gathered his children for this 1962 family portrait outside their Upper Kalskag cabin. Dan is the young boy at left. *(Photo courtesy Ausdahl Family)*

In 1979, Dan's parents opened a store in a lean-to attached to the cabin. From canned goods to motor oil to frozen pound cake, the inventory was squeezed into what many would consider a front porch. Sales helped support the couple's church work.

In 1990, when his parents were ready to retire, Dan and his wife, Dora, bought the store. The following year, they expanded and moved into a new building overlooking the Kuskokwim.

In the village, using a steambath is a typical way to get really clean—from the inside out. Called "taking a steam," the old-style Native method of bathing has changed only slightly from ancient times until now. Long ago, men built a fire outdoors and heated rocks, then moved them into a small sod hut and poured water on them. The bathers would sweat in the hot, steamy air, then they'd rinse with clean water before going outside to cool off.

When Dan was a boy, the method had been adapted: the fire started inside a low, stick-built enclosure with a mud floor and a smokehole on top. Dan remembers seeing steaming figures cooling in −20°F winter air, looking like they were on fire.

"Now we have a nice steamhouse with a waiting room," he says. In the second room, bathers can hang their clothes and cool down afterward before going outside. The Ausdahls' family steamhouse, big enough for two or three, is outside their backdoor.

"Normally, every other day, we take a steam, or if you've been out working and sweating and tired . . . If you've got sore muscles, it'll work on your back, your muscles, tendons, whatever. It's very good for you—a really healthy way of taking a bath." ■

Sweat, Lather, and Rinse

THE STEAMING AREA is 8-by-10 or 8-by-12 with a 4-foot high wall, so that contains the heat and the steam that you need. It's no more than 4 feet at the eaves on the outside measurement, which brings the inside down to 3½ feet. There's a wall there with a door where you exit into the waiting room (cooling room, dressing room) where you can cool down. That's 6 feet high at the eave so you can stand up. Mine was 6 x 6 x 8, so you can comfortably sit down and cool down.

You have your options for heating the rocks: you can have a woodstove, an oil stove, a gas heater, or whatever. It's pretty elaborate now. The way I've built them is the simpler way. You're just using natural wood to heat your rocks, so you're not burning any fuels.

Let the fire burn for twenty minutes or so. Leave the draft open, so it'll create a heating fire, so it'll burn and heat the rocks at the same time.

When the fire is how hot you want it, you put the metal bucket in front of the opening so it closes it. As the fire burns and heats the rocks, it's heating the water. The water will be pretty much come to a boil by the time you're ready. (You don't want to pour cold water on rocks because they can explode.)

You undress and go in there. The more water you pour on the rocks, the hotter it's going to be.

—*Dan Ausdahl*

For the stove, you use a 55-gallon drum. Prior to using it you burn it out so there's no paint or metal stuff in there. Cut an opening in the front where you'll put the wood in and cut it to fit whatever metal bucket you're going to heat water in. I like to use stainless steel that can hold 5 or 6 gallons of water.

The rocks go on top. We put the rocks in wire fencing to hold them on top of the stove, so they don't go sliding down. Look for a really smooth rock with no pores in it. It can be a light rock or a darker rock. If you don't take a smooth rock, they'll start exploding on the stove. Maybe fist-sized or smaller. If they're too huge, they'll take too long to heat. Use a water dipper with a long wooden handle to spill hot water over the rocks (like a fruit cocktail can on the end of a yardstick handle).

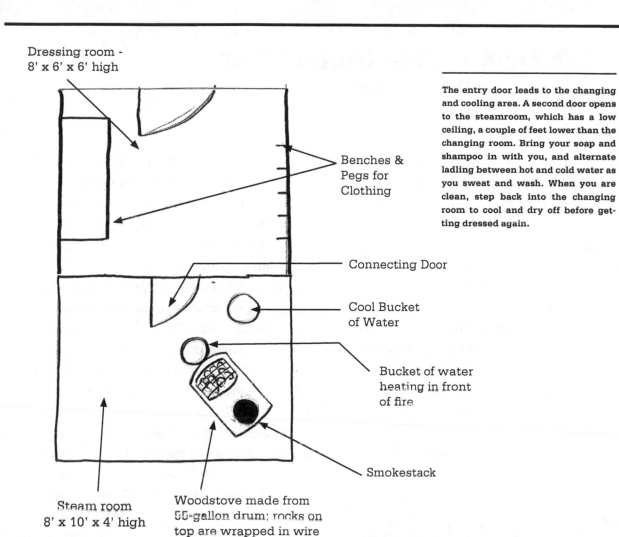

Dressing room -
8' x 6' x 6' high

Benches &
Pegs for
Clothing

The entry door leads to the changing and cooling area. A second door opens to the steamroom, which has a low ceiling, a couple of feet lower than the changing room. Bring your soap and shampoo in with you, and alternate ladling between hot and cold water as you sweat and wash. When you are clean, step back into the changing room to cool and dry off before getting dressed again.

Connecting Door

Cool Bucket
of Water

Bucket of water
heating in front
of fire

Smokestack

Steam room
8' x 10' x 4' high

Woodstove made from
55-gallon drum; rocks on
top are wrapped in wire
fencing

Inside the steambath, rocks are wrapped in metal fencing to secure them upon the barrel woodstove. Bathers use homemade dippers to spill water on the heated rocks, filling the small room with steam. *(Photo courtesy Ausdahl Family)*

13 How to Age Game Meat

SETH KANTNER, Kotzebue
Alaska-born in 1965

Like so many other children of pioneers, Seth Kantner is a product of his parents' decision to break away from mainstream USA and head for Alaska. Howard and Erna Kantner had both grown up in Ohio, but had moved independently to Fairbanks in the 1950s. They met at the university, fell in love, and married. Soon they would move even further from the mainstream.

Seth and older brother, Kole, were raised in a sod hut above the Arctic Circle, at a home so remote that the boys most often could only dream about what it was like to have friends, the kind they read about in the books that came by mail. They called their parents "Howie and Mama," what they heard the adults call each other.

"I think we were isolated enough that we weren't aware of what other people were doing," he says. "We were weird in many ways."

The solitary life was his father's idea, and northwestern Alaska was his region of choice after seasonal work brought him there during a critical time in the territory's history, in 1958, when the US Atomic Energy Commission (AEC) was developing an idea to use nuclear bombs to blast a harbor near Point Hope. Plans did not include the advice or consent of the local Iñupiat people. Seth's father was a biologist's assistant studying caribou on the Chukchi Sea coast during the "Project Chariot" years.

"He quit his job there when he met an Eskimo couple living in a sod igloo on the proposed blast site, there at Cape Thompson, and he lived the winter with them," Seth says. "The man had one leg and the woman taught [Howie] to hunt. He hunted everyday for them and their dog teams. He liked that lifestyle."

By 1962, with Project Chariot under heavy scrutiny and public protest, the AEC announced that it would "defer further consideration." Eventually, it was scrapped.

As for the Kantners, Erna deferred to her husband's desire to live a subsistence lifestyle far from community—about thirty river-miles downriver from the village of Ambler. They managed to get to town a couple of times each winter when Seth was young. As the boys grew older, they went more often.

Seth Kantner was born and raised in the Bush, and still lives in Alaska's far northwest, where he writes, fishes commercially, and carries on a subsistence lifestyle with his wife and daughter.
(Photo courtesy Seth Kantner)

"It might have been kind of romantic going North with this guy," Seth says. "But having kids in this cavelike place . . . She was always more physically affected by the winter darkness."

Both Seth and Kole went on to earn university degrees, and while Kole resettled in Seattle, Seth's sense of home led him back to Alaska's northwest. In 2004, he gained national literary acclaim with his first novel, *Ordinary Wolves*. And in 2008, he released a memoir titled *Shopping for Porcupine*, in which he writes with gripping honesty about his youth.

"My mom missed people and light and the freedom of cars," he wrote. "In the winter she stared south at noon at the orange horizon and waited in quiet anguish for the sun to return. Our dad was from a city, too, yet that somehow made him love this silence more."

Seth is a husband and father today. He's worked as a trapper, fisherman, gardener, mechanic, igloo builder, and adjunct professor.

His stories and photographs have appeared nationwide, evoking imagery of a life that's unique to most readers, including most Alaskans.

"It was no credit of mine, no breaking trail," he says. "I was just born into it." ∎

Young China Kantner lends a hand in skinning a musk ox. *(Photo courtesy Seth Kantner)*

Tips for Tender Meat

A BIG PART OF LIVING OFF THE LAND, and connection to the land, is food. Especially meat. I see a lot of people that come and spend time out and bring granola bars and bags of trail mix from Costco . . . I feel like they're missing out on the connection.

Taking care of meat is something that is done poorly by most people. It's fairly straightforward—it's just skinning and gutting the animal, and keeping the meat very clean and dry. Then cooling it. And aging certain parts.

I'm talking about parts you plan to cook as steaks and roasts—from moose and caribou and musk ox. Animals like beaver and rabbit, goose, lynx, porcupine all generally are great fresh and cook well if they are fat.

The main thing about meat is how you shoot it and what you do afterwards. Well, the main thing is that it's fat! A chased animal doesn't taste as good as one that's shot when it's not fleeing for its life. After an animal's dead, I like to skin it out and allow the meat

Tips for Tender Meat (cont'd)

to cool. Of course, in midwinter, you're working in the opposite direction; you're trying to keep the meat from freezing. In above-freezing weather, I skin the animal and butcher it into as large of pieces as I can handle. The muscles need to tighten against the tendons and later relax. If you bone-out your meat into a cooler or Hefty® bag, like some of the headhunters do, all that meat tightens up like rubber bands. You also have that additional surface area to go sour and let the flies get into.

I bring the animal home whole. I gut it out and often leave the lungs in it and take the stomach out and the intestine and the throat—so it's clean—but the lungs are still in there, adding to the warmth, and the animal's still covered with its own fur. On a long snow-machine ride home, the meat will still be warm.

I pretty much like to age all meat a little bit. With bear you hope it's marbled with fat and in that case more forgiving when it comes to cooking. I hang the meat the first night. The idea is to try to get it down to 50° to 60°F the first night, and then to 35° or somewhere around there for as many days as possible. Ribs, leg bones, and soup meat I'll put away in a day or two—in the freezer if I'm not upriver. Meat for soup doesn't need to age as long for tenderness. (Liver we fry directly after getting caribou, and tongue and brisket we generally simmer that first evening.)

The backstraps and tenderloins, and roasts and fry meat off the quarters tastes better and better the more it ages. It keeps getting more tender. You don't want to be wearing out your jaw like frying meat the first night off a caribou. Cooking; cast iron is important. I fry meat hot and fast, let it finish on the table in the pan so it doesn't get overcooked. Roasts I sear and then cook as low as possible for hours in the Dutch oven. Put a chunk of fat in. Don't add any water. Cut your meat so each roast has a bone. Meat without a bone we fry or dry. Give a hunk of meat with no bones to some of these elders, and they're going to wonder why you're so stingy.

In the Dutch oven, make sure your roast doesn't get "wet." Water comes out of the meat. Especially after it has frozen. Tilt the lid occasionally until it simmers back down to just a little juice simmering in the bottom. You want

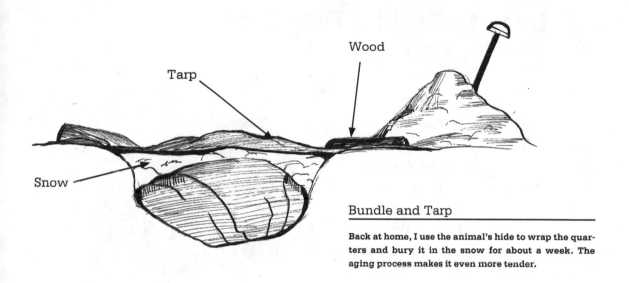

Bundle and Tarp

Back at home, I use the animal's hide to wrap the quarters and bury it in the snow for about a week. The aging process makes it even more tender.

a beautiful roast, not something that tastes like tough dry liver. Too much water will do that. Soup is a different story.

In midwinter, I'll quarter a moose or musk ox if I have to, but bring caribou home whole. If you have a 5-, 10-, 20-mile snowmobile ride, keeping it whole helps keep that meat warm. In the middle of winter, if you shoot a caribou, the meat's warm and the fur is protecting it. I gut it out and often leave the diaphragm and lungs in—to hold more warmth. I leave the skin attached to the animal, but separate the skin quickly in the Eskimo method—with your fists, down the ribs and sides. Then I wrap it in a tarp, and put it in the sled.

At home I'll dig a hole in the snow, lay the tarp in there, finish skinning the caribou and lay the hide fur-down, skin-up, in the hole. I'll put the butt half, shoulders, and probably the backbone in. Ribs on the side—they can freeze whenever—they are for soup. Fold the hide over your meat. Bury it with snow. The softer the snow, the better the insulation. Of course, I'm going to throw a tarp over the top and maybe some firewood, to keep the foxes from digging down in there. Your meat will stay thawed for at least a week. In the process, that meat ages and becomes much more tender, much more flavorful, and makes good steaks and good roasts. If you're out in the wilderness, you can slowly let it freeze, or if you end up with a warm spell, you just dig it up and bring your meat out and let it freeze in the air. As it ages, the meat just keeps getting tastier. Well, until it starts to get old. Then it's spring and hopefully fat geese are showing up.

—*Seth Kantner*

14 How to Build a Dog Team

JEFF KING, Denali Park
Alaskan since 1975

When somebody refers to the "King" in Alaska, they're not talking about Elvis. It's Jeff King, a name known not just in Alaskan dog-mushing circles, but around the world. He's Alaska's "winningest" musher, having finished first in more middle- and long-distance races than any other competitor.

For several decades, Jeff has bred, trained, and raced champion sled dogs on the Husky Homestead, an orderly scattering of buildings and doghouses across a spacious spread in the middle of the state. Fairbanks is a couple of hours to the north; Anchorage is several hours to the south. There, his three daughters grew up near the boundary of Denali National Park and Preserve. Summers on the Husky Homestead are peopled by visitors who arrive for a guided tour through the kennel and a storytelling session with the champion himself. Winters are snowbound and hushed, except for the barking riot that breaks out when Jeff or one of his handlers is choosing dogs for a run in the woods. No one wants to be left behind.

Jeff was nineteen when he landed in this area on June 9, 1975, ready to take on a summer job at what was then Mount McKinley National Park. He and three other California college kids came north on the Alcan in a Chevy pickup, trading off on driving and sleeping in a marathon trip. They arrived in the Interior near midnight, and the sun was still bright enough to read by.

Jeff King takes a team of young dogs, called a "puppy team," for a training run in fall 2011.
(Photo courtesy Husky Homestead)

"I was hooked on Alaska," Jeff wrote later in his book of trail adventures titled *Cold Hands, Warm Heart*.

He stuck around that winter, lodging in a tiny cabin. One of his few neighbors was Dennis Kogl, a dog-team freight hauler for Mount McKinley climbers, and Jeff was impressed by the man and his well-trained dogs. A year later, Jeff acquired his first sled dog, an animal shelter rescue named Angie that his brother brought up from California. With Angie, he began his experiment in mushing, building a sled from old skis, adding select dogs, and living in a wall tent on the trapline. He upgraded sleds as his dogs responded to training, and gradually Jeff developed a strong team.

"After three months of what I initially considered just an enactment of a childhood dream to live a subsistence lifestyle, I had a healthy dog team, a small sack full of marten pelts, and had survived the Alaskan cold of winter with simple, basic equipment," Jeff wrote. "Although it was not a life I would choose to live forever, those three solitary months forced me to consider a direction in my life. It also was an advanced education in the behavior and capabilities of the remarkable Alaskan husky."

A few years later, Jeff was ready to stake his own homestead. In 1979, he built a modest log cabin that's still standing today as an outbuilding among several on the Husky Homestead. In the decades since his first race, Jeff has also proven himself a worthy competitor on the trail, winning the Iditarod Trail Sled Dog Race four times, and crossing the finish line first in the Yukon Quest International Sled Dog Race. A dozen other wins in middle-distance races secured his position as one of Alaska's top mushers.

We asked him how he goes about choosing dogs for his competitive teams. ∎

An innovative King training technique involves the installation of a running wheel in the puppy pen, allowing the youngsters to indulge their natural love of running whenever they feel like it. *(Photo courtesy Husky Homestead)*

Born to Run

Q. *What are the physical differences between a sled dog and a house pet?*

A. A house pet does not describe a dog to me—it describes a place they live. You can turn a husky into a house dog if you don't let him out of the house. Many people have very athletic pets and house dogs, and they can make great sled dogs. But as you might think, it depends more on what we do with them after the day begins.

Physically, sled dogs have a metabolism and a fur coat that is comfortable in cold environments. There are many people who talk about their pet husky, they just can't believe it, he goes out and lies in the snow! He's quite fine there. They recognize that their house pet has some of these traits such as sleeping out . . . or their husky house pet, he keeps sneaking out of the fence, digging under it, and he runs far. What should I do about it? The dog's trying to tell you something. He wants to run, and you're not helping him by keeping him in the house.

Q. *How many dogs are needed to run a trapline?*

A. Historically people would take just one dog, and they would walk on snowshoes. The dog's job was to carry the gear.

I ran a trapline with four or five—that's a great number. They don't go real fast, but you don't want to go fast when you're

Born to Run (cont'd)

trapping. You need dogs that won't mess with your sets and won't mess with your furs. When you stop, you need them to not be a problem, barking and digging and making a big commotion. You need them to lie down, stay put, and behave throughout the day. Like the UPS man driving from house to house, he parks his truck. You need to go from set to set and park the team. They can't be scaring all the game away by barking, tearing up the trail.

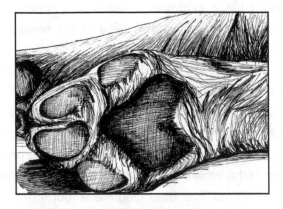

Mushers pay close attention to their dogs' feet. They strap on fleece booties for long-distance racing, as running for long periods on snow and ice can harm their pads.

Q. *What are their positions, and strengths of each position?*

A. Assuming there are more than five dogs:

- LEAD DOG—somewhere between twelve to eighteen months, I feel like I usually have an inkling of a superstar.

- SWING DOGS—two that are directly behind the leaders. They're up-and-coming leaders that are probably listening to the commands and are probably prepared to take a shot at the leader job sometime soon. The term was used with oxen or mules. If you were turning your stagecoach, the leaders led the way, but you needed more help to swing the team.

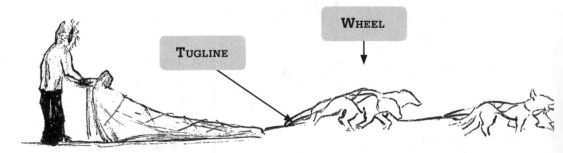

- **WHEEL DOGS**—run in front of the sled.

- **TEAM DOGS**—all the dogs between wheel and swing.

Q. *How do you teach verbal commands?*

A. You reward wanted behavior and discourage unwanted behavior. When they go to the right when you say "Gee," you say "Good dog!" And when they go to the left when you say "Haw," you say "Good dog!" They want to be rewarded, therefore they will learn to do the things that you reward them for. First you have to understand what the individual dog thinks is a reward. Some need verbal congratulations; others may need a food treat. Those are the two most common rewards.

When I trained my first lead dog to verbal commands, I used a bicycle, a harness, and a rope. I had enough power with the brakes, my bike, and me, I could stop. When I said "Gee" and he went to the left, I stopped. And he figured out that that was not working—he was confused, looked around, and then tried something else. He tried to the right, and I said, "Good dog!" He figured out, "I'm being rewarded by continuing to go." Most of the time, that's the biggest reward. If you stop them from running, you're discouraging the behavior that they want. Soon they learn, "He'll let me run if I go this way."

Q. *What's the most important thing to remember?*

A. In my mind, it's becoming familiar with what the dog's thinking. Until you know what they're thinking, you have a difficult time figuring out what your behavior should be to get them to do what you want them to do.

—Jeff King

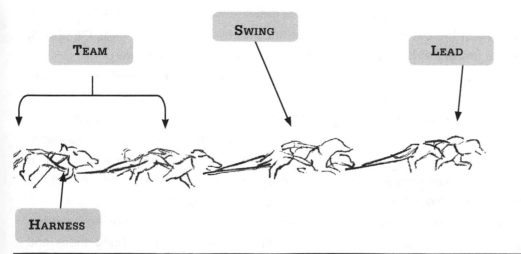

TEAM   SWING   LEAD

HARNESS

15 How to Operate a "Bush Maytag"
LYNETTE CLARK, Fox and Central
Alaskan since 1975

Lynette quickly learned how to run heavy equipment, and she partnered with Dexter Clark in both marriage and mining. *(Photo courtesy Lynette Clark)*

Among the gold-mining folks of Alaska's Interior, Lynette Clark is known as "Yukon," short for "Yukon Yonda." Back in September 1975, the adventure-seeker pulled up stakes in Illinois and headed for Fairbanks. For three years, she worked bartending and waitressing—at Pike's Landing, the Red Garter Saloon, the Stampede Saloon, the Chena View. Meanwhile, Lynette put out word that she was looking for gold camp work. Finally in spring 1978, she got a job cooking for a crew on Harrison Creek. The Circle Mining District lay roughly 150 miles north of Fairbanks.

"That first season mining was a trial by fire," Lynette remembers. "One guy on crew was a sexist pig who was always 'at' me, until I invited him to look out the window of the cook shack. I pointed out the little white flowers and identified them as hemlock." With that, Lynette gave the man an unveiled warning to lay off—that as camp cook, she could give him a roaring case of diarrhea without sickening anyone else in camp. And it worked.

On laundry day, Lynette would take a truck into the tiny town of Central, where the roadhouse owner let her use an old wringer washer he'd set up out back.

"He had run a hose and an extension cord to this wonderful convenience," she remembers. "The clothesline was nearby, as was the bar, the restaurant (somebody else's cooking), the phone, and the television . . . it was heaven."

This was a step up from Lynette's most rudimentary—yet effective—method of washing clothes: a five-gallon bucket and a plunger.

"I told the crew members my deal: I'd wash, hang dry, fold, and deliver clean laundry, but I'd get to keep the fine gold that washed out of the really 'mucky' work clothes."

Typically, after washing and rinsing the white bedding and underwear, she'd hang them and start the next load. But instead of draining the tub, she'd add another cup of soap and next run the dirtiest load—the work clothes. Only afterward did she drop the drain hose and partially drain it.

"With about two to four inches of water remaining, I'd turn the machine on its side and scoop out the residual mud on the bottom of the tub. That material was put into a jar for panning once I got back to camp. That first season I got almost a full ounce of fines."

At the end of season, Lynette hitched a ride to the annual miners' party at Arctic Circle Hot Springs, thinking she'd put out feelers for a better-paying job next year. Headed into the lodge, she met another miner, Dexter Clark. Later on, after playing three rounds of pool—which Lynette won—the pair commandeered a piano bench to talk. She needed a job; he might have an opening.

"He was tired of his own cooking and the time it took away from mining," she remembers. "But, could I cook?"

The next morning, Lynette was in Dexter's camp, whipping up a sumptuous breakfast for his crew. She was immediately hired for the 1979 season.

At the new camp, she announced the same deal with laundry—she'd get to keep any fine gold. That would make a sweet little bonus. Then there was the day that Dexter showed up with a Maytag Model N, the Chieftain, which in 1940 could be ordered with a gas or electric engine. This one had been an electric model.

"When Dexter brought that thing down the creek to camp, of course I commented that we

didn't have electricity," Lynette says. "He said that was okay because that part was broke anyway. With a couple of pulleys and fan belts, he hooked it up to a three-horsepower Briggs and Stratton pull-start motor. At first the pulleys were on backwards and it was spittin' socks out of the wringer at about thirty miles an hour! He reversed them, and it ran fine at a reasonable rate for washing."

After years of mining together in the Alaska Bush, Lynette and Dexter took on a mining job with a sure payday: demonstrating modern mining ways to thousands of visitors each summer. When they parted ways, "Yukon" stuck with the tourism industry, demonstrating gold panning at Gold Dredge No. 8, north of Fairbanks in the Goldstream Valley. Dexter went back out to his claims on a remote creek. Both are the real deal—bona fide miners who know what it's like to

In the summer of '79, "Yukon Yonda" found work in a mining camp as chief cook and laundress, but she also helped with camp chores like mixing cement for constructing a shower. *(Photo courtesy Lynette Clark)*

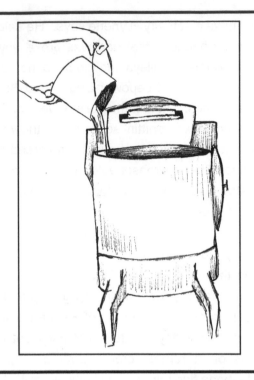

Fill the tub with clean water using a hose or bucket. Start washer and add soap.

Make the first load the "cleanest" dirty clothes; ease in laundry a piece at a time. When wash has ended, drain and refill tub for rinse cycle, then run articles through wringer, adjusting pressure for thickness of each piece, and hang to dry. Drain tub and repeat. Or reuse water on your next load—the extra-dirty clothes. If you don't have electricity, then you can always use a plunger and a wash tub!

push tons of dirt and sift it for little yellow rocks. As partners, they had both run the heavy equipment, but it was Lynette who gave the camp her special touch: doilies and wildflowers on the cook shack table, platters of delicious food, and squeaky-clean work clothes.

If you're not willing to use a washboard, but want to get back to basics on laundry day, Lynette suggests you search the Internet or local antique stores for a reliable workhorse. In fact, Maytag's Model E, or Master, was in production longer than any other wringer washer, from 1939 all the way until 1983. Other makes and models will serve well, too. ■

While pushing dirt always put a smile on Lynette's face, running it through a sluice box was always the stage that made her heart flutter. (Photo courtesy Lynette Clark)

16 How to Build an Outhouse

DOUGLAS COLP, Southeast and Interior Alaska
Past President, Pioneers of Alaska, Igloo No. 4 and Grand Igloo
Alaska-born in 1914 – died December 24, 2010

Doug Colp hunted rabbits to eat during the winter of 1935–36. The young man from Petersburg lived in a sod yurt at College, Alaska, and paid $5 a month in rent to University of Alaska president Charles Bunnell. All so he could advance his education in minerals and mining engineering. One day he would teach at that very university, sharing what he'd learned from a long and successful career in mining, one that has not yet ended.

"I'm still involved in the mining in the Central area," he said in 2008. "Too old to quit I guess."

Born in Petersburg in 1914, Doug was raised on a fox farm outside of town, and spent many boyhood days roaming local rivers with his gold pan in hand. His father was a prospector, fisherman, welder . . . a general jack-of-all-trades, Doug says.

"Every year he used to take us out for a couple of weeks camping, and most of the camping involved panning and sampling rocks, looking at them, discussing them, and so forth," Doug remembered. "He got me interested. The only two things I was ever interested in were mining and forestry.

"I had my fill of fishing; I could see there was no future in it. I was on the cannery tenders, on the seine boats, and the halibut boats. I fished for about everything you could name, but I didn't feel that I wanted to do that for the rest of my life."

During winters at college, Doug and three other students would ski sixteen miles round-trip

Known more for his skills in mining than building outhouses, Doug nonetheless offered good advice on setting up camp. The dredge bucket in front of his house came from the dredge he worked in the late 1930s. *(Photo by Tricia Brown)*

to dig for gold, leaving on a Friday, working all weekend, and skiing back on Sunday night.

"We got a lot of exercise," he remembered. "No fancy skiing, but what we called 'good strength and awkwardness.'"

The men worked an existing claim, melting the frozen soil, and creating a mound of earth that they hoped held gold. They wouldn't know until the season changed.

"In the spring of the year, we sluiced what we took out in the winter," Doug said. "We paid all our bills and our 10 percent royalty, and we were able to split a couple hundred dollars."

In summers, Doug worked for the Fairbanks Exploration Gold Company at a dredging operation out of Manley Hot Springs. And in 1940, he graduated with a bachelor of science in mining engineering.

"The school was pretty small at that time," he said. "But there were more mining engineers graduating that year than there are graduating today with 10,000 in the school."

In the decades that followed, you could point to just about anywhere in the Interior, even as far north as Prudhoe Bay, and Doug probably had a hand in investigating its potential for gold, oil, or gas. Many weeks of every summer were spent in a remote camp. And for a decade, from 1965 to 1975, he taught at the university in the Minerals and Petroleum Technology program.

Doug and his wife, Marcel, celebrated sixty-seven years of marriage in 2010. She claimed she was still learning new things about him. He said the handful of vitamins and minerals he swallowed everyday—at Marcel's insistence—were why he'd lived such a long and healthy life. That and so many hours outdoors.

"She helps me stay healthy. I tell people I'm on the pill."

In the Colps' Fairbanks yard were a couple pieces of mining history: gold dredge buckets that spill over with colorful plantings in the summers. These hold personal history, too: they're from the dredge that Doug worked as a college man.

"That's been a derelict dredge now for sev-enty years," Doug said. "I was on there for 1938, '39, '40, when I was going to school, summertimes. Finally, I was able to get two buckets from that dredge, so that made her happy. They call 'em flowerpots now."

After many years of camp living, Doug offered the following directions on how to build an outhouse. ■

Doug joked about building one- or two-holers (in case you want company). Most are one-holers, and depending on the house owner, could be decorated or left plain. This one had a stained-glass window above the door. *(Photos by Tricia Brown)*

First, You Dig a Hole

IT'S PRETTY SIMPLE. You got to keep your outhouse away from the other buildings, 50 feet or 100 feet. You dig a hole in the ground, how deep depends on long you're going to be there. If it's a long time, it should be 6 to 8 feet deep. You build your house over the top of that. You can have one-holers or two-holers or whatever you want, in case you want partners.

You want ventilation a bit. It should be fairly tight for mosquitoes and so forth. You can use a net inside if you have to. To keep the stench down, you can use lye, once a week or so, and that kinda purifies everything. It's got a Chlorox® effect.

Your outhouse is usually just a slanting roof, very simply built, the front a little higher than the back. Use a tin roof or plywood with roofing paper on top. Most of the old houses had corrugated tin roofs.

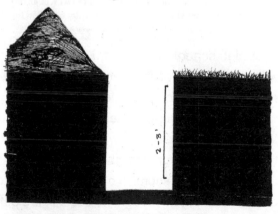

The number of people in the camp—and how long they plan to use the facility—should determine how big a hole to dig. The house itself is a basic four-sided affair with a door and good ventilation. For a toilet seat, choose from cutting a hole, installing a store-bought seat, or use a ring of Styrofoam® (works well in cold temperatures).

Squirrels love to shred toilet paper. Keep yours safe and dry in a used coffee can with a secure lid. You might even put a rock on top of the lid to keep the varmints out. Keep a bag of lime (calcium hypochlorite) in the outhouse and sprinkle some down the hole every so often to cut down on stench.

You've got to have a can for the toilet paper, with a rock on top to hold it down so squirrels can't capsize it.

Newer methods, after Styrofoam® came out, we always tried to use Styrofoam® seats, so you're instantly warm when you sat down. Before that was wood; you made it smooth so there were no splinters.

The half-moon for ventilation, with a screen over it, it's one of those symbols that indicated outhouse, I guess. I don't recall, the ones I've built, that I've ever used that. It's little bit more trouble than I wanted to go through.

In a shorter-term camp, you'd only dig two to three feet, depending on how long you have to be there. It should be deep enough to bury it when you leave.

Mine were all short-term, mining camps, prospecting camps. But sometimes you have twelve to fifteen people, so you have to dig it deeper—depending on how much usage it's going to have. With one or two men you wouldn't even need one—you could put a hole between two trees.

—*Douglas Colp*

17 How to Catch a King Salmon

KEN MARSH, Matanuska-Susitna Valley and Anchorage
Alaskan since 1966

Ken Marsh was four in 1966 when his young parents came north from California for a teaching job with scant pay. So hunting and fishing wasn't for sport; it was all about feeding the family.

"To make ends meet, we would go down to the Kenai [Peninsula] and get tons of salmon to freeze," Ken says. "We hunted caribou every year, and moose. I don't remember having my first beef-steak until I was in about fifth grade. I remember it was so tasty that I ate it all and got sick."

As a boy, Ken learned about gun safety and shooting, and got his first caribou when he was eleven. He even ran his own trapline on week-ends. As for fishing, well, he helped put food on the table and had a good time doing it. The fall

Above Right: Ken Marsh tested his physical limits on his agricultural homestead, clearing trees for home logs and firewood sales, before he decided to go back to school and get a degree. *(Photo courtesy Ken Marsh)*

Below Left: In 1979, Ken was running his own trapline as well as hunting and fishing (for food and for sport). He discovered this massive moose rack in the woods, and suspected that the animal died naturally or following a battle with another bull. *(Photo courtesy Ken Marsh)*

after high school graduation, Ken headed for the wilderness north of Trapper Creek, where he and a friend trapped for a couple of seasons.

In his early twenties, Ken would get a piece of the Alaska dream himself with a 160-acre agricultural parcel through the state's land lottery program. Ken was to submit a business plan to grow a crop, something he thought he could figure out. He and a friend started clearing the land, selling the firewood and house logs. They labored day after day, cutting and loading wood onto flatbed trucks.

Ken was living in a wall tent and sleeping in a bunk made from saplings. One day after a hard, sixteen-hour stretch of bucking logs and making deliveries, he lay in his sleeping bag, physically spent, when a bear came calling.

"Even though I was in good shape, every muscle in my body just burned. And that's when I was young!" he remembers. "Then I heard something just outside that canvas. It's not very thick, and I heard almost like a pig snort right in my ear. I sat up, picked up my shotgun, stuck it outside the tent flap, and I just went Ka-boom Ka-boom! And he went crashing through the trees. I didn't even get out of bed."

In snowy November, Ken upgraded from the tent to an old homesteader's cabin. Then, one day in December, when the days were short and the flatbed was fully loaded, it got stuck up to its axels. Ken thought, "You know, maybe I should consider continuing my education." He tabled his project and went back to school, studying English and journalism.

Right out of college, Ken was hired at the Valdez newspaper, then a month later, he accepted a job offer that would set the course of his career: outdoors editor at *Alaska* magazine.

Through Ken's expertise in fishing, hunting, and trapping, coupled with his gifts in writing and photography, Alaska's wild places have been opened to a national audience. After many years at the magazine, he wrote *Breakfast at Trout's Place*, a critically acclaimed book, then began a long-running fishing column in Alaska's biggest newspaper. Meanwhile, more articles were appearing in dozens of national outdoors magazines. In 2008, Ken was featured on the Outdoor Life Network, and joined the Alaska Department of Fish and Game, a rare melding of work and play. ∎

A Fight to the Finish

KINGS ARE THE FIRST salmon to run each spring. They begin arriving in some rivers (especially those of the Copper, Kenai, and Susitna drainages) as early as late April, though runs don't really get started until late May or early June. Runs peak in most regions around the end of June.

Kenai River kings average 30 to 65 pounds, but probably the best size for handling is 20 to 30 pounds. Every cast is a roll of the dice. And there's no real way to screen for larger or smaller fish when casting with rod and reel. Large fish will sometimes take tiny baits or lures, and vice versa.

Many favor a heavy bait-casting rod-and-reel combo. The rod (graphite construction is considered best by many) should be built for monofilaments lines between (roughly) 18- and 30-pound test. The reel should be able to accommodate 150 yards of 25- or 30-pound test line.

Many kings have been caught on lighter, less expensive gear. Something along the lines of an old Fenwick or Eagle Claw medium-weight fiberglass rigged with a Mitchell 300 open-face reel and 20-pound test line will catch kings—though will be put to test.

Some elite anglers use fly tackle, but the bread-and-butter rigs of the masses include plugs, spoons, spinners, and baits. Top plugs

A Fight to the Finish (cont'd)

are KwikFish®, sometimes used in conjunction with sardine strips tied to the plug's body. Top spinners include large Vibrax and Teespoons. Pixee spoons are an ol' tried n' true spoon. Baits of cured salmon roe are often fished under corkies or hanks of brightly colored yarn. Herring, cut plug-style, is effective for catching kings when trolling in saltwater.

I look for kings holding in the tail-outs of large, deep pools and in eddies close to shore or behind boulders. Cast far enough upstream, and include enough weight on your line to allow your bait or lure to sink to the bottom where kings hold. Don't add too much weight—you want your offering to be light enough to bounce along the bottom with the current.

Strikes vary from light taps to lightning-bolt grabs. It depends on the fish and the situation. Either way, be ready to haul back fast and firmly to set the hook. Hang on, keep constant tension on the line (not so much that it breaks!), and let the fish wear itself out against your grip, the rod's spine, and the current. When the fish begins to tire, you'll be able to lead it into shore where a friend should be available to scoop it up with a landing net.

—*Ken Marsh*

KwikFish® are a favored plug among king-salmon anglers, sometimes used in conjunction with sardine strips tied to the plug's body. The rattling noise from a Pixie spoon is said to attract kings.

Ken bagged this monster in 2011, dragging it out of a river in South-central Alaska's Susitna drainage. *(Photo courtesy Ken Marsh)*

18 How to Read a River

KAI BINKLEY SIMS, Bethel and Fairbanks
Alaskan since 1980

ay "Binkley" to a Fairbanks resident and the word-association answer is "Riverboat Discovery." That's because there's been a Binkley running a tour boat on Fairbanks-area rivers since 1950, when Kai Binkley Sims's late grandfather, Captain Jim Binkley, bought the *Godspeed* and launched what would become Alaska Riverways, Inc.

But the family's history on Alaska rivers goes back yet another generation to Kai's great-grandfather, Charles M. Binkley, who built and skippered riverboats on the Yukon and many of its tributaries, the Susitna, and the Stikine Rivers, during and after the gold rush. Charles died in 1923, when his son was a preschooler; Jim would

Jim and Mary pose with their four children in this 1960s photo aboard the *Discovery*. All three sons would become licensed riverboat captains. Kai's father, John, is at right. *(Photo courtesy Mary Binkley)*

enter the trade later, working with his uncle on the Stikine.

Captain Jim's three sons—John, Jim Jr., and Skip—grew up to be riverboat captains, as have several of his grandchildren. Kai's father is John Binkley, who raised his family in Bethel and conducted a tug and barge business on the Kuskokwim River while keeping ties to the Fairbanks operation.

For six decades, generations of Binkleys have led cruises on the Chena and Tanana Rivers, teaching Alaska history and Native culture to hundreds of thousands of visitors. Nearly all of them were passengers on a riverboat named *Discovery*. The first *Discovery* was designed and constructed by Captain Jim himself. *Discovery II* was bigger, wider, and taller; *Discovery III*, four decks high, can transport 900 passengers.

Enter Kai Binkley Sims, who at one time was the country's youngest female stern-wheeler riverboat captain. The Coast Guard licensed her in 1998, after hundreds of hours in the wheelhouse driving under a licensed captain, and the required written test and charting test. Kai earned a 100-ton Master's License, one step away from that required for skippers of cruise ships and tankers.

In 2002, Kai graduated from the Colorado School of Mines with a bachelor's degree in petroleum engineering and was immediately hired by BP in Anchorage. Later, she married and started her family, putting both her master's license and her degree on the shelf—for the time being.

"There's really no pressure in my family to be involved in the business," she says. "Right now, I'm not involved much in the daily operations, but hope to have my kids grow up working in the family business just as I did. It's a very fun and intense job in the summer, of course."

Running the riverboat everyday is not like driving a truck on the same stretch of highway, because so many variables affect the water, Kai says. You choose the "lane," or "channel," that's right for that day.

"Reading the river is not something you can learn from a book; it is a skill that's passed on from one generation to the next," she says. "It's a lot about getting a feel for the river."

The *Discovery III*'s river highways—the Chena and the Tanana Rivers—couldn't be more different. The Chena is a freshwater stream, with clearer water and defined banks. The Tanana is the largest tributary to the mighty Yukon River and is fed by massive glaciers at its headwaters. Its water is milky-colored with sediment called "rock flour," literally rock ground so fine that it is suspended.

At the confluence of Chena and Tanana, the swirls and eddies make beautiful patterns in the water, like a huge dollop of cream has been poured into a giant's coffee cup.

Both rivers are an important part of Fairbanks history, too. In 1901, city founder E. T. Barnette booked passage on a stern-wheeler named the *Lavelle Young*. His intent was to ascend the Tanana to a place called Tanana Crossing and establish a trading post. Relying on a tip that the Chena was a shortcut, Barnette urged the captain to take it. But it was too shallow. When the captain felt he could go no further, he offloaded Barnette and his goods on the bank and wished him well. That place would become the Fairbanks we know today. ∎

In the photo at left, Kai's grandfather, Captain Jim Binkley, assists passengers aboard the *Godspeed*, a twenty-five-passenger boat that he and wife, Mary, had purchased from the Episcopal Church mission at Nenana. With it, the couple began the sole "employees" of their new business. *(Photos courtesy Mary Binkley)*

Messenger in the Water

THE TANANA IS A BRAIDED RIVER and it's continually changing, depending on the volume of water moving. If it's high water from lots of runoff and glacial melting, then the channel looks completely different than it does at low water. The Tanana isn't charted and the channels can be different from one day to the next. That's why we have to rely on reading the river, rather than on charts.

A fast-moving river like the Tanana is difficult to read because of the glacial silt suspended in the water. The Chena River is fed by rain runoff and snowmelt, so it's easier to read. The water moves slowly, and the channel doesn't change dramatically from day to day.

Usually when you're going around a bend, most of the deeper, faster water is on the outside of the curve. The water moves slower on the inside, and that's where you tend to get sandbars. The slower water doesn't have the energy to keep the sediment suspended, and it will accumulate and make the water shallower.

So where the water's moving the fastest is usually the deepest channel, but that's not always the case. If it's low water, it can look completely different than if it's high water. Another tool for finding the deep water is to watch where the drift is running . . . logs and debris in the water.

When the water runs over the river bottom, a signal is reflected in patterns on the surface. These patterns, or ripples, can mean different things. They can indicate the type of material the riverbed is composed of, or the depth of the channel. The wind can change these patterns and should be taken into account. Learning to read these patterns is an art and takes many years of practice.

—*Kal Binkley Sims*

A braided river (left) is broad and has many channels, some of which are very shallow. The skipper must read the water and decide which route to take.

A meandering stream (right) has a single channel, and the banks as well as the water's surface inform the skipper. The cut bank, the outside bend in a river's course, is where water is moving faster, and usually is deeper. Other patterns suggest hidden hazards. When you're in a small boat, it's good to know if there's a log or something sticking up. It can be a V-pattern on the surface.

19 How to Put In a Winter Water Hole

JOE RUNYAN, Yukon River
Alaskan since 1971

The Alaskan term "Bush rat" applied to Joe Runyan for most of his years in the North. After graduating from Oregon State University in 1970, he arrived for a summer float down the Tanana River from Fairbanks to the Yukon River. Once he landed at the village of Tanana, Joe adjusted his plan. He decided to stick around that fall to hunt moose. Instead, he stuck around for good.

"I met a really remarkable Athabascan guy named Freddie Jordan, and he became a very good friend," Joe says. "He was born on the Yukon in a cabin in 1948, the same year I was born in Oregon. I trapped one winter and went on many sled-dog expeditions with Freddie. He was an incredible outdoorsman. I learned a lot from him."

Joe fell into the seasonal rhythms—fishing, hunting, and trapping with his dog team. He spent months alone on the trapline. Summers, he'd go fishing, then back to the woods as the seasons changed.

"We trapped back on the headwaters of the Blind River, and the Nowitna River . . . ," he says. "At that time there was kind of a back-to-the-land movement. A lot of people had the idea, but I found out later that not a lot of people actually did it.

"When I got married, we'd float down in the fall from fish camp with a load of fish on top of a big wood raft," he remembers, "to about seventy

Worn out but exhilarated, Joe Runyan finished the 2008 Iditarod Trail Sled Dog Race on March 15, fourteen years after retiring from racing. Nearby, Tim Osmar and his wife, Tawny, who had loaned Joe a dog team, were there to welcome him. *(Photo by Jon Little)*

miles below Tanana. We'd beach the raft, unload the fish, the dogs, everything we had, and set up camp. As the water went down, the raft got dry-docked on the beach. And that was our winter wood."

At Christmas, the Runyans would come into "town," one of the remote villages of Tanana or Ruby, then return to winter camp.

"When you were at those camps—there wasn't a lot of them out there—you'd hear who was living out by Huslia, who was on the Porcupine . . . It might be years before you met them, but you knew them."

In the early 1980s, Joe grew interested in dogsled racing. And when the kids were school-aged, the family moved into Nenana, a small town on the road system. Joe developed his kennel and did well in middle-distance races, then entered the thousand-mile Iditarod Trail Sled Dog Race in 1983, finishing eleventh in his rookie run. Two years later, he took first in a new race, the Yukon Quest, and in 1989, claimed the Iditarod championship, making him the first to win both long-distance races.

In the mid-1990s, Joe stopped running and adopted a new role, that of race commentator, author of *Winning Strategies for Distance Mushers*, and consultant for documentary filmmakers.

In 2008, Joe was back on the Iditarod Trail when he was invited to accompany Oregonian Rachael Scdoris, a legally blind woman. Although Joe was nearly sixty and didn't have a dog team, musher Tim Osmar, who'd been sidelined, loaned him one. Their teams made good progress until Rachael scratched at Koyuk. Joe should go on, they agreed, and he arrived in Nome to a hero's welcome, fourteen years after his last Iditarod finish. Reporting for race sponsor Cabela's, Jon Little wrote:

"Under the thick fur ruff and dark glasses, he busted loose with that trademark Runyan grin and made one point crystal clear: 'This may have been the last Iditarod with Joe.'"

Joe offered the following Bush-living tip on how to have fresh water all winter long. ■

After several years of placing well in middle- and long-distance races, in 1989, Joe won his Iditarod championship. *(Photo courtesy Joe Runyan)*

"Running" Water at -50

THE YUKON, TANANA, IDITAROD RIVER—any of those fed at their headwaters with silty water from melting glaciers—will run clear under the ice of winter. The glaciers start to freeze up, so all that runoff water isn't in the rivers. By far, river water tastes better than melted snow or ice. In addition, it takes a lot of firewood to melt snow, and there's spruce needles in it and rabbit droppings. You don't want to melt snow to drink. And you don't want to be packing ice from a river or lake. It's a good alternative when you need it, but ice always has grit and sand in it that blew in while it was freezing up. You want to get river water.

Any river, as it freezes, will go through a couple of stages. First it'll be throwing ice for three or four weeks in October and grinding ice will make a constant background rumble.

Before the river freezes, look for slack water, an eddy, right close to your camp. That's where you'll chop your hole when the ice drops.

"Running" Water at -50 (cont'd)

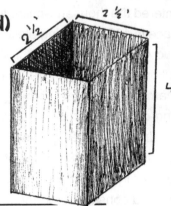

All of a sudden in the middle of November, it'll be silent, so quiet, and the river's frozen. Standing water at the margins along the banks will gradually freeze.

When you see there's overflow on the sides, you're not ready to put your water hole in—you want to wait. After the creeks that feed the big rivers are frozen, you'll stop getting the big water flow. The ice will drop—it always does—and when it drops, all that ice on the sides of the river will be caving in.

That's when you go out with your ax and chop your water hole in about half a foot of ice. In advance, make your liner out of old boards or even split spruce poles (see illustrations). You put that four-foot, open-ended box down in to your ice hole, and situate it so it freezes in place. Sometimes you have to kick in some snow around the box like mortar until it's frozen solid in the hole. Cover the top of the box with a canvas or boards or spruce boughs and insulate with snow. Even at -50°F, the water hole will be open. By the end of the winter, the

Get some old boards and make about a 2-½-foot-by-2-½-foot box with both ends open. Just make four sides with some boards. The Yukon's going to freeze about 4 feet deep in the winter, so you make it 4 feet long. Put the liner into your ice hole. Obviously the wood is going to go below the bottom level of the ice. Let it freeze in place.

ice could be four feet or more on the Yukon.

The ice always freezes in from the bottom. People that don't line their water hole are always chipping ice out of a hole they've chopped. It gets smaller and smaller at the bottom, and by midwinter it isn't even worth the effort to chop the ice. Then it's back to melted snow and spruce needles. But with that box, the water stays open all the time. Sometimes you have to knock a couple inches of ice off the surface—that's all—and you and your dogs have plenty of water.

—*Joe Runyan*

Cover it with a piece of wood or canvas, and kick some snow over the top. Even if it's been fifty below, you can open it up and you'll have water down there. It won't freeze in from the bottom.

20 How to Lay a Woodstove Fire
OLE WIK, Kobuk River Valley
Alaskan since 1962

The Kobuk River Valley was Ole Wik's destination in late 1964. He'd already earned two degrees before serving two years in the military, based in Anchorage. That summer, he was working at McKinley National Park, with plans to head Outside in the fall for doctoral studies. But there at the park, Ole met a couple who would influence the direction of his life. Keith and Anore Jones had spent the previous winter along the Kobuk River, living in a sod hut they'd built themselves.

"I was entranced," Ole says, "and wanted to accompany them on their return in the autumn. But what about the fellowship and that whole career path? I agonized. Ultimately . . . I couldn't force myself to give up Alaska."

In the village of Ambler, he met Keith's brother and his wife, Mike and Sally Jones, who were building a sod house using small trees and saplings. Like others, they'd been inspired by another transplant to the area, Oliver Cameron, who'd built an underground house using a few hand tools and raw materials from the forest. Ole built near the Joneses, about three miles downriver from Ambler.

"I had gone into the Kobuk with very little in the way of material goods," Ole says, "and wouldn't have been able to make it without their support, loan of tools, etc. But I did design my own sod hut, quite different, much smaller."

Ole and son Kalle on the tundra in 1976. A small fire heats soup after a successful caribou hunt.
(Photo courtesy Ole Wik)

Hurrying to beat the snow, Ole chose four straight trees for uprights and connected them with four top logs to form a nine-by-eleven-foot box. Next he cut saplings and leaned some of them against the frame for the walls, and placed others on top for the roof. Finally he covered the entire structure with heavy plastic sheeting and backfilled with excavated dirt to ground level and as high up the walls as possible. Blocks of moss were then placed against any exposed plastic in the upper walls, and two layers of moss covered the roof. Come winter, snow would add another layer of insulation. Mylar sheets served as small windows.

The expense? That first hut cost all of $26 for the plastic sheeting, plus a few dollars for nails and staples. And he found enough steel in an oil drum for a tight stove.

Looking back four decades, he recalls those years as "living close to the bone."

"Bear in mind that I grew up in the city," he says, "had never built anything, and had never even lit a woodstove. Nevertheless, over the years Manya and I built three more semi-subterranean dwellings, fed our family by rifle and nets, found a way to make a living, and home birthed our kids."

For the next few years, the Wiks did not stay in one place for long. They moved on to jobs in Katmai, Glacier Bay, and Australia, before pursuing educational goals in Hawaii. By 1969, oil had been discovered at Prudhoe Bay, and Ole's old job at Glacier Bay had reopened. He jumped at the chance to return, as he put it, "while Alaska was still there."

Next, a return to the Kobuk River Valley and a new sod hut heated with another homemade woodstove. Those first few stoves were just a beginning. He went on to make all kinds of stoves, large and small, as described in his 1977 classic *Wood Stoves: How to Make and Use Them.*

The family left Alaska in 1985; afterward, Ole returned North for fourteen summers to build airports in remote villages. ∎

In this 1969 image, Ole's wife, Manya, was at work peeling structural support logs for their sod home in progress. *(Photo courtesy Ole Wik)*

Light My Fire

FIRE-STARTING REQUIRES DRY WOOD, so it is a good idea to have a box of kindling tucked away. Everybody has his own way of laying a new fire, and here is mine. Place two splits of dry wood on either side of the firebox, say three or four inches apart. If there is any old charcoal among the ashes, arrange it so it lies between the splits. Next lay some shredded paper on the charcoal. (Newspaper is ideal; avoid glossy paper such as that found in catalogs and magazines. It doesn't burn uniformly.) Lay the kindling on top of the paper, and place a few small splits of wood on top of the kindling. Now light the paper and close the stove door. Open the draft just enough to encourage the fire without blowing it out. Once the stove is drawing well, add as much wood as the situation calls for.

Another way to kindle a fire is to use sawdust moistened with kerosene or stove oil. Place a couple of spoonfuls of the sawdust mixture among the kindling sticks, in place of the newspaper. Light the sawdust

Another option for a quick start is to make a "fuzz stick," with cuts along the wood to allow air to circulate.

with a match, and you'll have an instant, trouble-free start-up. I should not have to add that gasoline or other explosive substances should never be used in stoves. The danger is obvious, yet I know a man who burned down a fine log house in this way. Also, never add kerosene to anything but a cold stove, since the heat may vaporize it, forming an explosive white cloud that could flash back in your face.

Purists like to start fires without resorting to newspaper or petroleum products. One good way to do so is to carve a fuzz stick from a piece of kindling. Put it in the firebox in place of the paper, and light the wood shavings with a match.

—*Ole Wik*

Left: If you have some charcoal in the ashes from a previous fire, arrange them between two splits. Layer shredded paper, then kindling, followed by smaller splits on top.

21 How to Identify Edible Berries

VERNA PRATT, Anchorage
Alaskan since 1966

Verna's passion for Alaska's native plants has spread to others through her classes, guided field trips, and many books. *(Photo courtesy Verna Pratt)*

Uncle Sam moved Verna Pratt and her husband to the Anchorage area in 1966, two years after the historic Good Friday earthquake shook Alaska's footings with a monumental 9.1 on the Richter scale. When the Pratts arrived, services and transportation had been restored, splits in downtown streets had been mended, and buildings had been torn down or repaired. But the earth still rumbled with occasional aftershocks, creating the greatest unease among those who'd experienced the big quake. Even so, when Verna's husband was discharged from the Army, the couple decided to stay.

One day, when Verna had a notion to make some jellies, they went looking for berries, and she realized she'd have to learn what was edible and what was not.

"Everything was different here," she remembers, her Massachusetts girlhood still accenting her words.

Verna had no idea that a need for berries would lead to a fascinating hobby and further develop into a consuming career. In a few decades' time, she became an authority on native plants, from identifying them, to collecting and growing them from seed, to teaching classes, leading field trips, and writing books on the subject. She also founded the Alaska Native Plant Society, attracting others to her infectious hobby.

"It came from food use, and it just grew," Verna says, adding that many surfaces inside her home are covered with plants in various stages of growth. And there's the greenhouse, too.

Although Verna was self-taught, she did take some lessons in plant nomenclature, and she now teaches plant identification through the Alaska Geographic Association and the Murie Science Center. Her groups are limited to a maximum of ten students at a time.

As for her own ramblings around Alaska in search of plant life, she's been to Prudhoe Bay, Nome, Circle, to Southeast Alaska, Valdez, Kodiak, St. Paul, and Unalaska. She's trundled up the Yukon's Dempster Highway, and down the Alaska Highway through Canada.

"Not everywhere, but pretty much," she jokes.

If there's a Holy Grail of Alaska native plants, it would be *Douglasia ochotensis*, the Alaska dwarf-primrose, Verna says. It's the one plant that she hasn't yet seen with her own eyes.

"It's a little rounded plant with real pretty five-petal pink flowers. It gets so covered with flowers that you can't even see the leaves. It grows in some places on the North Slope and on St. Lawrence Island—real restricted places."

Verna's days can be filled up with marketing and selling books, and growing and selling plants, both important aspects of her work. But she's ready to drop it anytime for a trip into the wilderness.

"When I want to go, I just go," she says. ∎

CRANBERRY BARS

Sift together: 1½ cups flour ½ teaspoon salt
½ teaspoon soda ⅛ teaspoon cinnamon
Add: ¾ cup brown sugar 1½ cups quick oats
Stir in: ¾ cup melted shortening
Pack: ½ of the above mixture into an 8-inch-square pan

Cook until berries are soft:
1 cup cranberries ½ cup raisins
½ cup honey ⅔ cup water
Add: 4 teaspoons flour 6 tablespoons sugar

Cook until thickened. Cool and spread over mix in pan. Cover with other half of mixture. Press lightly. Bake at 350°F for 20 or 30 minutes, until lightly browned.

FRUIT LEATHER

Cook 1 quart rosehips with 1 quart highbush cranberries for ½ hour. Put through food mill. Add 1¼ cups sugar. Lay a sheet of plastic wrap on two cookie sheets, clipping wrap to side of cookie sheet to keep edges from falling into leather. Spread mixture on sheet. Place in oven on lowest temperature, keeping door ajar. Dries in 3 to 5 hours. Remove from plastic and roll when done.

Highbush Cranberry

Choosing Correctly

Currant

- BLUEBERRY (*Vaccinium*) leaves are oval to ovate, flat and usually not toothed at all. Also, usually the end of the berry is mostly flat.
- JUNEBERRY OR SERVICEBERRY (*Amelanchier*) leaves are broad, rounded at the end, and distinctly toothed. They also are slightly folded at the mid vein. The end of the berry has remains of sepals.
- CURRANTS (*Ribes*) have leaves similar to a maple leaf and placed alternate on the stems.
- HIGHBUSH CRANBERRY (*Viburnum trilobum*) leaves vary from top of the stem (almost oval) to the bottom of the stem (similar to a currant) and are opposite on the stems.
- BOG CRANBERRY OR TRUE CRANBERRY (*Vaccinium oxycoccos*) has small pointed evergreen leaves and thin stems trailing on the ground. Oval berries on a thin curved stem.
- LOWBUSH CRANBERRY OR LINGONBERRY (*Vaccinium vitisidaea*) has rounded, curved, glossy evergreen leaves on thick upright stems with bunches of berries on the top of the stems.

—*Verna Pratt*

Blueberry

Juneberry / Serviceberry

Bog Cranberry

Lowbush Cranberry / Lingonberry

22 How to Build a Cache

TOM WALKER, Denali Park
Alaskan since 1966

Tom Walker seems to have lived enough to fill three lives, from bronco buster to log-home builder to nature photographer. *(Photo courtesy Tom Walker)*

Tom Walker had sampled life around Alaska—briefly dwelling in Fairbanks, Anchorage, and then the Alaska Range, Loon Lake, and Homer—before the early 1980s, when he found a three-acre parcel in the very heart of the state and built a small log home. He had built a couple of other houses along the way, but at this one the rolling stone came to a halt.

"The 1970s was the era of the *Mother Earth News* looking like a phone book," he remembers, "and Earth Day was big, and the return to the land, and *Roots*. I think it was a blowback from the Vietnam issue and the way our country was going. I was not doing this as a reaction to all that; it was rather something fundamental that I've always wanted to do."

Today, Tom is regarded as one of Alaska's premier wildlife and nature photographers, whose superb images have appeared in scores of books, periodicals, and calendars worldwide. But as a kid, he was an L.A. boy with a heart for the wilderness. He wanted to be a farmer or a rancher someday—anything that would take him into the wild spaces, where he loved to look for birds and animals.

"I was the world's biggest nerd, chubby, in my own la-la-land world," he remembers. "I loved adventure stories of Africa and Alaska. And nobody took me seriously."

In his own brief adventures, Tom was seeing sights that he could only describe back at home. But no one believed him. So he started taking pictures with an inexpensive camera.

"I got into photography so no one would call me a liar," Tom says. "I would bring back pictures of a giant buck mule deer, or a black bear, or a

The cache was a typical outbuilding for cabin dwellers, who needed a high place to store their goods. *(Photo by Tricia Brown)*

California condor, and I would show them to people and it was, 'Golly, maybe the kid wasn't lying after all.' It was evidence."

When he grew older, Tom found work at various ranches, which drew him into the High Sierras. Next came a stretch as a cowboy on the rodeo circuit—riding bulls and bucking horses. He gained fair scores and near death from a cracked neck vertebrae on at least one occasion.

"I got stomped . . . it comes with the territory," Tom remembers. "I got hurt pretty bad. And I did one more ride after I got hurt. I did really well and then walked away from it."

After a stint with the military, Tom decided to make Alaska his home, and eventually landed in the Denali Park area.

Describing himself as "a voracious searcher of old books on skills," Tom had studied the fundamentals of log-cabin construction. He worked with a competent builder out of Fairbanks, and continued learning on the job. Years later Tom would write *Building the Alaska Log Home*, considered a classic today, many log cabins and caches later.

"The first cabin I built on my own here was 18-by-20," he says. "The biggest log house I ever built for anyone was 2,000 square feet; which is way too big, but that's what they wanted."

In time, Tom's bad back—likely, old injuries from the rodeo circuit—coupled with the aftermath of cancer surgery forced him out of construction and further into photography. He still lives in a cabin that he built with the primary help of his friend Kim Blair, a master builder. Meanwhile his work as a professional photographer and writer continues to gain prominence. And though Tom's fans see his photos as fantastic works of art, he's very pragmatic about it all.

"The real reason I photograph is not for the end itself, for the photograph," he says. "It's a way to be outdoors, and it's a way to be able to pay for it. I have no artistic illusions. If I could be around animals all the time without taking pictures, I would do it." ■

Tom left the rodeo circuit and considered new career options after getting badly busted up. *(Photo courtesy Tom Walker)*

Arctic Refrigerator

CACHES ARE KIND OF A FADING ASPECT of Alaska; now that we have modern refrigeration, they're not quite as common as they once were.

There were two traditional types of caches. One was where you just lop off a tree fifteen feet off the ground, climb up there, put the cross-pieces on, and put a tent or tarp up there. You'd wrap metal around the legs or hope the bears didn't get up there. That was temporary. The wind would blow that over eventually.

The other style was, you essentially built a little cabin with four legs that you'd access with a ladder. In a solely practical sense, it doesn't have to look like that—but it doesn't

A cache is a small cabin atop stilts, with legs wrapped in metal, originally designed to keep animals, large and small, from gaining access to stored food and furs.

hurt because its original purpose was to be built as protection from bears.

First you put up the legs, then put up a platform base on top of the legs that have been sunk in the ground three or four feet, maybe more. (Old-timers sometimes sawed off trees at height for one or more legs. Not the preferred method.) The legs can then be cross-braced with cable and turnbuckles if necessary.

If you're going to build the cache out of logs, or poles, you construct it on the ground without nails or spikes or anything. You mark the logs, disassemble them, and reassemble them like Lincoln Logs on top of the legs. Some people put on a sod roof and that's fine, but you just want a good waterproof covering.

With framing materials, you'd prefab a bunch of it on the ground, then take it apart and reassemble. The secret here is to build the side walls in short sections so that they can be lifted to the cache platform by hand, then nailed together. Pre-built sections that seem moveable on the ground suddenly become unmanageable when lifted to height. Short is good.

—Tom Walker

This historic cache stands in Pioneer Park, Fairbanks, among many structures that were preserved and moved to the park in 1967. (Photo courtesy Tom Walker)

23 How to Keep Moose Out of the Garden

ANN D. ROBERTS, Fairbanks
Alaskan since 1951

Nearly all Alaska gardeners face a common foe, especially in late summer as you begin to consider whether to bring those big, beautiful broccoli heads in and get them into the freezer now, or let then grow a couple more days.

Enter that awesome, lumbering, ubiquitous ungulate, the moose. We love to see them in the wild, to watch them walk down the streets of our

Frustrated with the lack of accurate Alaska gardening information, Ann Roberts turned to those Alaskans who have spent their lives studying and working the soil in the state's varied and unique gardening conditions. She published her findings in her book, *Alaska Gardening Guide*. (Photo courtesy Charles Mason)

subdivisions or relax in urban parks. We especially love showing them to visiting relatives; but when they come to munch our carefully tended garden crops, it is war!

Growing crops in Alaska is a unique challenge due to the state's short summers, extended daylight hours, and cool soils; in some areas, permafrost lurks a very few inches below the surface. When Ann D. Roberts, of Fairbanks, decided to grow a garden, she was frustrated with the lack of information specific to Alaska. So she decided to write a book, pulling together Alaska's best gardening information from all the most reliable sources—successful gardeners from throughout the state, and the latest research of local horticulturalists. Her book is titled *Alaska Gardening Guide*.

Gardening was not really new to Ann. Her family first came to Alaska in 1951, when she was seven years old. A year earlier, her father had been sent from their home in Long Island, New York, to Ladd Air Base near Fairbanks.

"As soon as my dad got to Alaska, he decided that this is where he wanted to be," Ann remembers. "So he called us up and told us we were all coming. I think my mom and he were pretty much on the same page."

In a few years, Ann's family purchased 300-plus acres of land that had been homesteaded on Badger Road near Fairbanks.

"At first we lived in a tent, and then moved into

what we called 'the dark house,' because it had no windows. We lived there and began to build the basement of our home. When completed, we moved into the basement and continued to live there until I grew up and left home—then they built the house."

Ann's father had the goal of self-sufficiency through living entirely off the land. They built a barn, raised dairy cows, and grew a vegetable garden. All five children helped their parents to achieve that lifestyle.

"I gardened as a child, but only because I had to," she says. "I didn't like all the work we had to do for subsistence. Plus, the root cellar was full of spiders, and I didn't even want to go down there."

Aside from working in the vegetable garden, the children gathered the berries grown in the garden as well as what grew wild in the surrounding area.

"Our parents would give me a couple of cans and say, 'Don't come home until you've got them full.'"

In later years, when Ann married, she did not garden for a while. Eventually, she took a Masters' Gardening class; but as she began to consider her own garden, she became frustrated at the lack of Alaska gardening information.

"I subscribed to *Organic Gardening* magazine, and they ran an article about how great it

Ray and Darlene DeVilbiss of Palmer protect their lush vegetable garden from moose with two strands of electric fencing. They use one-inch white tape-styled material to create a hot, highly visible boundary that moose can easily see, and hopefully touch, before attempting to enter the garden. *(Photo by Nancy Gates)*

was to grow your plants under black plastic, but that's simply not true for the cool soils of Alaska. So I wrote an article about that, and they published it."

As Ann continued to search for accurate Alaska gardening information, she decided that others might benefit from her research, and she began to write her book—a collection of solid information gathered from Alaskans studying and working the soil in the state's unique gardening climate. ∎

Managing Marauders

MOOSE ARE FAMOUS FOR barging right through chicken-wire fencing and helping themselves to your best produce—usually the night before harvest. It is a common struggle for Alaska gardeners—and one that's difficult to win.

You can erect a high chain-link fence, with the posts anchored in cement. That solution, while generally effective, is expensive.

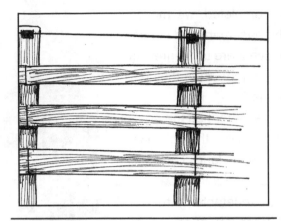

A less expensive, yet often effective option, is made of a single electric wire strung above a more visible fence made of wood, chicken wire, or a variety of other standard (or creative) fencing materials.

An effective, though expensive, option for keeping moose out of the garden is a high, chain-link fence.

A second option is a high rail fence made of sturdy wood; the fence must be high enough to discourage the moose from jumping over and sturdy enough to prevent them from "riding it down."

A wooden rail fence may also have a secondary, slanted fence leaning against it from the outside. This combined configuration may cause the moose to think twice about eating your broccoli and cabbage.

One of the most effective and inexpensive fencing options is an electric fence. A single strand of lightweight wire (there are a number of types specifically designed for safe, effective electric fences) is strung on insulators about a foot above the top of a fairly high, ordinary fence. A "fence charger," sends sharp, pulsating jolts of high-voltage—but low amperage—electricity around the wire. The lower fence may be made of chicken wire, wooden pickets, or of a variety of other creative materials; its main function is to make your electric wire boundary more visible to the moose. Hopefully, the moose will see the fence, sniff the wire at the top, and get a surprising shock, sufficient to encourage him to browse elsewhere. Electric fencing supplies are readily available at building supply and feed stores. They may also be ordered from the spring and summer catalogs of large mail-order houses.

—*Ann D. Roberts*

24 How to Land a Bush Plane

HARMON "BUD" HELMERICKS, Colville Village and Fairbanks
Alaskan since 1940 – died January 28, 2010

Nationwide, the name Harmon "Bud" Helmericks was synonymous with Alaskan adventure during the postwar years, when the famed Bush pilot was churning out books such as *We Live in the Arctic*, *Arctic Hunter*, *Arctic Bush Pilot*, and *Flight of the Arctic Tern*. Bud was featured in *Time* and *Life* magazines, and later traveled the country on lecture tours. As late as 1969, by then a veteran pilot, big-game guide, and oil company consultant, Bud wrote *The Last of the Bush Pilots*.

At the age of ninety, Bud's movements were a little slower, his eyes a little dimmer. But he was still living independently with Martha, his bride of fifty-eight years. And when the discussion turned to his lifetime as an Alaska explorer, adventurer, homesteader, and master pilot, Bud's blue eyes grew steely, resolved, and passionate . . . like that strapping, twenty-three-year-old who came to Seward in 1940, looking for work.

"I enjoyed living in Seward. I've enjoyed every place I've lived."

Bud landed a job transferring freight from steamships to trains, but adventure soon drew the young pilot further North to Alaska's wildest expanses in the Arctic. For fifteen to twenty years, Bud says, his Cessna 140, the *Arctic Tern*, was the only plane flying over the North Slope. He also regularly traversed the Arctic by dog team—alone—for the simple joy of exploration.

The legendary Harmon "Bud" Helmericks shares unparalleled stories and adventures from his seventy years as an Alaska Bush pilot, adventurer, big game guide, explorer, oil company consultant, and homesteader. *(Photo by Natalie Gates)*

"Just to be there..." Bud murmured, his eyes focused on long ago.

In the mid-1950s, Bud and Martha chose a site on Anachlik Island, at the edge of the Arctic Ocean, to raise their family. Colville Village, as they would call their home site, began as a few tents surrounded by snow blocks. They learned the essentials of wilderness living from their nearest neighbors, local Iñupiat families.

"Beautiful people," remembered Martha. "They were actually our mentors. They taught us so much about Alaska."

The couple soon built a permanent home, a hangar, and other outbuildings. They fished, hunted, and flew freight—advising and assisting when Prudhoe Bay was first explored and developed. And they homeschooled their boys—Jim, Mark, and Jeff—though two of the boys went to Fairbanks for a portion of their secondary education. All three became accomplished pilots, hunters, scholars, and businessmen. One was even named a Rhodes Scholar.

The family's small business, the Arctic Tern Fish & Freight Company, eventually diversified into several multimillion dollar corporations, including Colville Inc., Brooks Range Supply, and the Prudhoe Bay General Store, now led by sons Mark and Jeff. Eldest son Jim still lives year-round at Colville Village, where he raised his family.

Bud had only recently retired from flying, grounded by his flight-instructor son, Jeff, following a yearly check ride. Bud recalled those difficult words from a loving son:

"He said, 'You know, Dad, you have an impeccable flying record of 34,500 hours with no accidents, no injuries to plane or passenger, but. . . now you're not staying current, and I think it's time to hang up your wings.'"

Those 34,500 hours were over some of the wildest, most rugged backcountry in the world— far from improved airstrips or any semblance of emergency response options. Bud's exemplary flying record was the result of a lifetime of careful planning, keen judgment. . . and occasional errors.

Following are a few tips for Bush landings— on gravel beaches or pack ice—from a master. ■

YOU LEARN ABOUT FLYING FROM MISTAKES. I've been lucky, I've had to land sometimes in the fog or the dark and you couldn't see nothing.

When it comes to gravel beach landings, you've got to realize that you can't see holes in a gravel beach. It's all gravel, and you've got to use your depth perception. You've got to be sure the light is steady—whiteout conditions and shadows, for example, can trick your depth perception. And there can be a six-foot hole in the gravel beach, with all the same size rocks, and you can go right into it.

You've got to watch your wind, too, because if you don't know which way the wind's blowing, and how fast, you're in trouble.

As soon as you stop rolling, get out and walk over the whole area you just lit on, and that you're going to take off on again. Don't ever trust a landing that you've not walked over.

I'd rather land on pack ice than a gravel beach, because of the smooth ice, and there are no holes like on a beach. Watch for color changes in the pack ice. The color indicates different depths, layouts, and textures of ice. Just keep your wits about you. Don't just go bustin' in and land. You'll get in trouble.

And for Pete's sake, don't go trying to move around after you get down safely. Get out and walk around. Tie your plane—to the ice— because of the wind. You dig a hole with your pocketknife, this way and that way (V-shaped) until they meet, about fourteen inches deep or

An Ounce of Prevention

so, and then you run your rope down one side and up the other. Be sure to point your plane into the wind. They're made to meet the wind head-on.

And if there's going to be a high wind, lift the tail up and prop it up on a block of ice or something, so it sits level and doesn't get any lift.

Gosh, you know, there are so many variables in landing. Don't ever get the idea you know it all.

—*Harmon "Bud" Helmericks*

You may need to tie your plane to the ice because of wind. You just dig a V-shaped hole with your knife (about fourteen inches deep). It's not too bad to dig. Then run your rope down one side of the V and up the other.

Be sure to point your plane into the wind; if it's a high wind, level the plane by propping up the tail on something—like a block of ice—to reduce lift.

When landing on pack ice, you've got to watch for color changes in the ice. Different colors indicate different depths, layouts, and textures of ice.

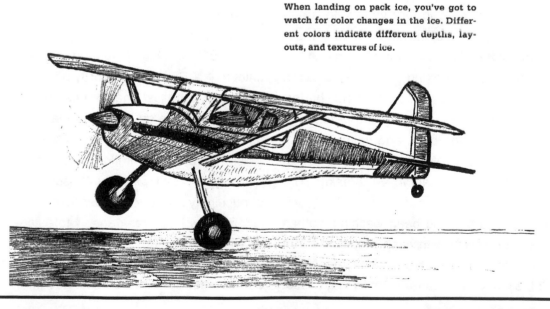

25 How to Build a Root Cellar

MAXINE DeVILBISS, Palmer
Alaskan since 1956 – died February 7, 2009

Ralph and Maxine DeVilbiss braved the long drive up the winding, narrow, bone-jarring Alaska Highway when they began their Alaska adventure in 1956. They brought along their three young children, Larry, Ray, and Susan, and an impressive assortment of backcountry skills— all of which would soon come in handy for their life in Alaska.

Ralph, raised on a farm in Oklahoma, was logging in the Pacific Northwest when an accident landed him in a Portland hospital, and in the path of his future wife, Maxine—a pretty, young hospital worker who delivered his dinner tray. Two weeks later, on Sunday, December 7, 1941, they had their first date and learned, over lunch, that the Japanese had bombed Pearl Harbor. They married six months later.

In their early years in Oregon, while Ralph worked at logging and farming, Maxine mastered many of the skills she would need on their future homestead: cooking and baking on a woodstove; milking a cow; churning butter; making cottage cheese; raising and butchering chickens, rabbits, and pigs; and doing endless laundry. Later she wrote about those years in her memoir, *Home-steading in Alaska; The Story of Wolverine Farm.*

"For two years, I had been washing clothes the old-fashioned way, with washtubs and a scrub board," Maxine wrote. "Sheets and greasy logging clothes were my bane in those days. Just

The late Maxine DeVilbiss recalls moving with her husband, Ralph, and their three young children to begin their lives in Alaska in 1956. They purchased and cleared land that is still being actively farmed by their children, grandchildren, and great-grandchildren. *(Photo by Nancy Gates)*

before Larry, the oldest child, was born, Ralph found an old wringer washing machine. Glory hallelujah!"

In 1956, the family headed for Alaska to volunteer at a Bible camp north of Palmer. It was supposed to be just one summer, but then Ralph found their place on Lazy Mountain. It was agricultural homestead land, available through the Alaska Rural Rehabilitation Corporation (ARRC). On July 21, 1956, he purchased two parcels, about eighty acres, for $5 per acre.

The raw land was densely forested—primarily with cottonwood trees, most of which Ralph soon cleared before he began planting potatoes and carrots. Once the garden was in, he started building the family's log cabin. At first the cabin was a single-story structure; a few years later he added a much-needed second floor. Near the house, Ralph dug a large root cellar into the side of a hill, confident that it would be needed come harvesttime.

For the next twenty-two years, Ralph and Maxine farmed the rich soil of their Wolverine Farm, supplying fresh produce to local grocery stores as well as to the military bases in Anchorage. Over the years, they also welcomed two more sons by adoption, Brian and Billy, and cared for countless foster children.

Up until the day Maxine DeVilbiss passed away, she was still very much the matriarch of the famlly. The DeVilbiss land—now farmed by the couple's children and grandchildren—continues to provide quality produce, meat, and hay to Southcentral Alaska. The fresh produce from

The DeVilbisses cleared their land, planted their garden, and then built the first story of their log cabin. A few years later, a second story was added. *(Photo by Nancy Gates)*

their gardens is still stored in the family root cellar until it goes to market.

In 2008, the pioneer Alaskan gardener shared these details on building a root cellar. ■

After the Harvest

WE BUILT A **100-BY-40**-FOOT root cellar. It held three or four hundred ton of potatoes. It was dug into a nearby hillside—close to the house—with a Quonset hut set up on top of it for aboveground storage. It's still in use today.

The floors and walls were made of cement. Ralph was on the go constantly . . . clearing land, digging into the slope for the root cellar, pouring footings, putting up eight-foot plywood forms for the walls, and hauling Quonset material and bags of cement from Anchorage.

When the cement walls were finished, I spent a day painting them with water repellent, and then later I applied a second coat.

Ralph made the front part of the cellar into a shop, so he could back trucks in there and unload them or work on them. He made the front wall of the root cellar out of logs, like our house.

We delivered produce throughout the winter, all stored in our root cellar; that's why it needed to be big. When Ralph first built it,

After the Harvest (cont'd)

he put a place for a chimney pipe to go out and put a barrel stove in there. But we rarely had to use it, because that root cellar kept them warm.

In later years, our oldest son, Larry, put a cooling system in. At harvest time, if you put produce in there while the outside temperatures are still mild, it holds the heat, and so you have to cool it down.

Then if it gets too cold in the winter, you have to start the fire, and let the warm air circulate . . . You monitor it by simply going out every day and looking at the thermometer hanging inside the cellar. If it's extremely cold and windy, you check more often.

They put shelves in one corner of the root cellar . . . for the use of anyone in the family who wanted to store vegetables for their own use.

The DeVilbiss root cellar is commercial-sized by necessity, however most families are well served by a modest four-by-six-foot root cellar, often built in the corner of a garage, or beneath the kitchen floor. The University of Alaska's Cooperative Extension Service offers free plans for building your own root cellar. Look for them online at www.uaf.edu/CES.

—*Maxine DeVilbiss*

Many Alaska homesteaders protected their winter supply of vegetables by digging an adequate, family-sized root cellar into a hill near their cabin.

26 How to Handle Isolation
LESLIE LEYLAND FIELDS, Bear, Harvester, and Kodiak Islands
Alaskan since 1978

L eslie Leyland Fields's Kodiak Island home is perched high on a cliff overlooking the Gulf of Alaska. She lives there with her husband, Duncan, and their six children. In addition to mothering her sizeable and active family, Leslie teaches post-graduate level creative writing classes and runs a professional writing business, The Northern Pen.

But every spring since 1978, Leslie and her family load four months' worth of supplies—groceries, fishnets, livestock, toothpicks, furniture, building supplies, fuel, and a mind-boggling assortment of other items—onto a commercial fish tender and journey to their other life, a fish camp on Harvester Island off the northwestern coast of Kodiak Island. Upon arrival, offloading the supplies and hauling them from the beach to their cabin, the Fields family immerses itself in the physically challenging, unforgiving, often life-threatening grind and glory of commercial gillnet fishing for their family-owned business, Fields' Wild Salmon.

Leslie met Duncan while attending Cedarville College in Ohio. Before their engagement, Leslie visited Alaska for a sampling of her future summers, the communal life at his family's isolated fish camp on Bear Island (near Harvester Island). Duncan, his parents, brother, and sister-in-law, all lived together at the camp every summer with no electricity, telephones, running water, or other modern conveniences. Leslie was introduced to a

Leslie Leyland Fields, wife, mother, writer, teacher, and commercial fisher, takes a moment from her busy summer schedule on Harvester Island, near Kodiak, to share the realities of life at the family's remote fish camp. *(Photo courtesy Amy Summer)*

world of mandatory self-sufficiency. She witnessed the skills and strength needed to haul in heavy nets and pick fish while balancing in a skiff on churning seas.

When Leslie returned to the island for the next season, it was as Duncan's wife. She boarded a flight to her new home in Alaska and considered the resolve she and Duncan shared for their future:

"I planned to work in the boats with the men. Though the other two women in the family did not, Duncan and I were determined to share the work, to share our lives, not compartmentalizing into male and female. Yet I cried there in my seat while over the Canadian Rockies, with my face turned toward the window so my seatmate couldn't see. 'A fisherman I will become,' I wrote. I hated the taste and smell of fish [but] I loved Duncan, and I was ready for another life."

For the next nine summers, Leslie learned what her life choices required of her. Extracting their livelihood from the sea through long hours, exhausting work, and often-dangerous circumstances inevitably led to relational stress. Eventually Duncan and Leslie decided they needed to make a change.

"We have to move, Duncan," Leslie recalls saying. "We have to start over somewhere else, make our own place, a place for [our future] children, a place for us."

So in 1987, Duncan and Leslie began building a new fish camp on nearby Harvester Island. The couple first lived in a shed on the uninhabited island as they built their new house from scratch. The following fall, they moved into the house and became the seasonal residents of Harvester Island, Alaska, population two.

Leslie has written powerfully and beautifully about the dramatic struggles and sweet rewards of living in two worlds: the close church, school, and grocery store–line camaraderie of Kodiak Island and the stark aloneness and exhausting fish-sleep-fish routine of summers on Harvester Island. She has learned how to cope with feelings of isolation and shares the following. ■

When Leslie Leyland Fields first arrived at the her husband's family fish camp more than thirty years ago, the couple was resolved to fully share their work of commercial fishing, whether it was pulling in a skiff from the running line (top) or long hours of picking fish from a gill net in a skiff (bottom). *(Photos courtesy Rebekah Jenkins and Naphtali Fields)*

When Two's a Crowd

Q. *When you first married into an Alaska commercial fishing family, and knew you would be spending your future summers fishing the waters off Bear Island, what were some of your main concerns?*

A. To be honest, I didn't anticipate a lot of the challenges I would face. I was very young when I entered this life—twenty. I saw this faraway island, which in the 1970s didn't have any connection to the outside world, and I only saw the good things—the incredible beauty, the drama of the ocean and sky, the cleanness of it all.

Q. *What are some of the challenges you have faced over the years, and what part did your isolation play in it?*

A. Relationships are right there near the top of my "challenge" list. For years, with not another soul around, my husband and I discovered that living alone together on a remote island can be paradise or purgatory. In truth, it is some of both! When we got mad at each other, we couldn't stomp off to anyone else's house, or call our best friend for advice! We were totally on our own. We had to learn to negotiate our differences, give each other space to pursue individual interests and abilities, to give ourselves permission to not do everything together. We're much the stronger for it now, but the passage has been long and not always easy.

And you have to find a balance between physical labor—which is so much a part of your life when you do everything yourselves—and the other kinds of work and play that feed your soul, spirit, and mind. There are many times when we work almost nonstop, but it's crucial to make

Leslie Leyland Fields found that living on a remote island, with not another soul around, can be paradise or purgatory.

When Two's a Crowd (cont'd)

time even then for some kind of play, relaxation, meditation, some way to feed relationships and the other parts of yourself. If you don't, you'll burn out.

Q. *What are some coping techniques you've developed?*

A. One of the most important things I've learned is not to be a slave to the tyranny of the always-urgent. I try to make time in each day, in the midst of the house-building, net-mending, and bread-making to pursue other kinds of knowledge and skills. I've really enjoyed becoming a student of my environment, going off into the meadow or down to the tideline with field guides in hand, trying to learn as much as I can about the land and water around me. Gaining some knowledge of your world expands its physical confines. When you can name a flower in your field, a mushroom, you begin to know it.

Also, I bring my other "friends" to the wilderness—my books and music, which pull me into a community and a conversation that extends far beyond my particular time and place.

Q. *What other practical suggestions would you have today for someone headed out to a remote life—far from everything familiar?*

A. Be clear and intentional about why you're choosing this experience or lifestyle. Work together on articulating hopes, goals, and plans to achieve them with the others who are part of this venture. Make sure that everyone involved has a sense of ownership in the process.

Try living in a remote area in smaller doses before you take the big plunge.

While there, mentally extend that experience to a longer term. Be realistic about the challenges, and realize that, over time, they generally increase rather than decrease.

Find or create a community in the midst of your isolation however possible. Get to know your neighbors, even if they're five miles away. You'll need them at some point, just as they'll need you.

Maintain some real-time connection to the outside world—whether it's a satellite phone, a satellite connection to the Internet, a radio, or all three. You'll need a communication system for emergencies, of course, but even more than this, an ear to world events helps you maintain your world citizenship and will help you keep perspective on your own life.

Finally, be pragmatic. Take a break from your homestead when you need it—without guilt. Homesteading and wilderness living is not a competition to see who can survive the longest without human contact!

—*Leslie Leyland Fields*

27 How to Make Zucchini Bread

ROSE NABINGER, Yukon River
Alaskan since 1954

Rose Nabinger's cozy home in Palmer reflects her warmth and hospitality. But Rose has not always lived in such comfortable surroundings. In 1954, she and her husband, Don, traveled from the southern tier of New York State to a remote Yukon River village to serve as missionaries.

"I was a city girl," Rose says with a smile. "I came from the city to the Bush. Don and I were high school sweethearts. He went away to Bible school, and pretty soon I followed him out there. I chased him until he caught me!"

Rose says her father worked at a furniture factory, but "he had farming in his blood." Though city dwellers, the family enjoyed fresh eggs from their own chickens and fresh produce from their backyard-turned-garden during the Depression.

Apparently Rose inherited some of her father's farming blood. Vigorous houseplants bask in the sunny windows of her home, while tomato plants and other vegetables thrive in large pots on her deck.

Rose tears up when she speaks of the recent loss of her husband, who passed away just five days before their fifty-sixth wedding anniversary. She vividly remembers the day in 1954, when they flew into the Yukon River village of Kokrines:

Rose Nabinger checks the vegetables growing on her sunny back deck in Palmer as she reflects on the lessons she has learned, gardening and otherwise, from having lived and raised her family in Alaska since 1954. *(Photo by Nancy Gates)*

Rose Nabinger's Zucchini Bread

Combine and blend with a mixer:

    3 eggs   1 cup oil   2 cups water

Fold in 2 cups peeled and grated zucchini.

Add, gradually, the following ingredients:

3 cups flour	1¼ teaspoons salt
1 teaspoon baking soda	1 tablespoon cinnamon (or nutmeg,
¼ teaspoon baking powder	or a combination of the two)

Add ¼ cup chopped walnuts (dates or raisins may also be added)

Bake 1 hour (on center rack of oven) at 325°F, or until done and toothpick comes out dry. Recipe makes two large loaves. For muffins, bake for 23 to 25 minutes; makes about 2 dozen. Freezes well, when tightly wrapped, for up to two months.

"When we landed . . . nobody was there. And we'd flown all those miles without seeing any villages or anything. We landed on the river, because there was no landing strip. The grass was up to my waist as I walked along, and I thought, 'This is the most desolate place I've ever been.'"

Yet the Nabingers lived contently in Kokrines for three years with Don working as the local postmaster on weekdays and holding church services in their home on Sundays. Their cabin was large by most standards at twenty-two-by-thirty-two feet. They created cupboards, dressers, and food-storage shelving by stacking "gas boxes"—wooden shipping crates that each originally held two five-gallon cans of gasoline.

In 1957, now with two children, the Nabingers moved to Kaltag, another Yukon River community. The cabin was smaller, and their family grew larger during their seven years there. Besides his mission work, Don also served as the village medical aide. Sometimes he worked with guidance—transmitted intermittently via shortwave radio from a doctor in Tanana—but often without. "He learned from doing, and he did a real good job," Rose says with a note of pride.

Aside from his two jobs, Don kept busy hauling water from the nearby creek for bathing and drinking, and firewood to keep the barrel stove roaring when the winter temperatures dropped to -50°F. Much of his transportation was by dogsled. And with no refrigerator in the cabin, Rose says, her husband got creative.

"Don found that he could dig down through the moss to the permafrost, maybe eighteen inches deep," she remembers. "He put a metal box down in there, with a cover, and then replaced the original moss on top. I could keep milk and juices cold there in summer. It was like a root cellar; it was just small—maybe four feet by four feet—and right outside the house."

An actual root cellar, dug into a hillside near their home, protected their vegetables from freezing in winter. "It worked real well," Rose recalls. "It would be cold right close to the door, but way back into the hill, it was just right."

The Nabingers grew beautiful vegetables in those few inches of unfrozen earth in Kaltag. They made adaptations, like planting stubbier varieties of carrots. Rose also learned how to grow zucchini in Alaska's cool earth. She took that knowledge with her when she and Don were sent from Kaltag to work in an orphanage on Lazy Mountain in Palmer. ■

Growing Zucchini Alaskan Style

ZUCCHINI GROWS FINE out in the garden in Alaska. Some years, when it seemed cold, I would plant it, and cover it with clear plastic. When the plants would start to grow I'd cut an X in the plastic above the plant, and pull the plant up through it.

Planting vegetables in a raised bed encourages better growth by warming the Alaska soil.

Rose created additional warmth (and moisture) by covering her newly planted garden with clear plastic. She covered both edges of the plastic with soil, to hold it in place. When the plants sprouted, she would cut an X in the plastic and pull the plant starts through.

That keeps the warmth and moisture in. The weeds grow too, but they don't seem to grow as well when they don't have the air. And I dug a trench on either side of the row, and started the plants in kind of a raised row, put the plastic over, and covered both edges of the plastic with soil, to hold it down.

Alaska gardens don't produce as much zucchini as those in the Lower 48, but they produce well. If we even have six weeks of nice sun, they'll grow. I use the same recipe for zucchini bread or for muffins. Everyone says it's the best zucchini recipe they've ever tasted.

—Rose Nabinger

28 How to Grow Giant Cabbages

DON DINKEL, Past Grand President, Pioneers of Alaska
Wasilla, Palmer, and Fairbanks
Alaskan since 1937

If you're really curious about all things horticultural in Alaska, you won't have to dig very deep before you come up with the name "Dinkel." The Dinkel family has three generations of Alaska farming under its belt and, through diligent scientific research and practical experience, has become an expert resource on the subject. They also happen to grow giant vegetables, but according to Matanuska colonist and professor emeritus of horticulture Don Dinkel, that part is really "just for fun."

In 1935, as the United States struggled through economic depression, drought, and pestilence, President Franklin D. Roosevelt instituted the Matanuska Colony Project. The project gave 203 Midwest farming families a chance to rebuild

Don Dinkel, professor emeritus of horticulture at the University of Alaska Fairbanks, has a lifetime of experience in teaching, researching, and experimenting with all things agricultural in the state of Alaska. But each year he grows giant vegetables, like the cabbage above, "just for fun." *(Photo by Nancy Gates)*

Brenna Dinkel, granddaughter of Don Dinkel, competes in the Alaska State Fair Giant Cabbage competition in this 2009 photo. *(Photo by Nancy Gates)*

their lives on the fertile land of Alaska's Mata-nuska Valley, north of Anchorage.

The colonists were hopeful about their new lives, but the realities of a short growing season, high shipping costs, and distance to markets were among the many challenges that soon checked their enthusiasm. Many eventually decided to leave Alaska, and replacements were then selected and sent. The Dinkels arrived in Palmer as part of that second wave of "fill-in" colonists, arriving in February 1937. Don was five years old.

"When the opportunity came to move to Alaska, my family grabbed at it," Don says. "We lived—for a couple of weeks—in a tent near the railroad depot in Palmer. Then we were assigned to Tract 14, as far west as you could go in the Colony Project. Our farm bordered the Seward Meridian. After nine years, we gave up the Colony place, and Dad took up a homestead."

Following high school, Don left Alaska to earn his undergraduate degree from the University of Minnesota and, following a two-year military commitment, completed his doctoral degree there as well. He then returned home to help research and resolve some of the agricultural issues that challenged both the Colony farmers of long ago, and those farming Alaska soil today.

Don's lifetime of research and experimentation at both the Palmer and Fairbanks Agricultural Experiment Farms—and his years of teaching Plant Physiology at the University of Alaska Fairbanks—has had significant impact on Alaska farming. The Dinkel name is also legendary due to their success at growing giant, prize-winning vegetables for the Alaska State Fair in Palmer.

Today, Don helps his granddaughter, Brenna, grow her yearly entry into the mega-veggie competition. Brenna's most recent win was in 2005, when her cabbage tipped the scales at eighty-five pounds. ■

Infrared transferring film (IRF) warms the Alaska soil, but does not allow the photosynthesis needed for weeds to grow. Don Dinkel demonstrates how he cuts, then reaches through the IRF to plant cabbage starts. *(Photo by Nancy Gates)*

Growing Giants

ALASKA HAS A GOOD CLIMATE for growing food. Vegetables grown in Alaska have very high-sugar content, low-fiber content, and excellent yield. You can improve on that by warming the soil temperatures, so you can increase the growth rate.

I've used a lot of different methods, but the one that is the most practical for growing crops is plastic mulch. Not black plastic, because it does not warm the soil at this latitude. Clear plastic is better, but the best is called IRT (infrared transferring film). IRT transfers the infrared radiation to the soil and warms it up—usually by 20° to 25°F. But it doesn't transmit the visible rays needed for photosynthesis—so you don't get weeds growing. Raised beds help warm soil temperatures, too.

I usually till my soil down to about six to eight inches.

Most crops do best in a slightly acid soil, with a pH from 6 to 7 (6.5 would be optimal for most crops).

For giant cabbages, most people use special seeds, like O-S Cross. My granddaughter and I have been using a progeny of a cross between O-S and another big Japanese variety.

I start the giant cabbages indoors at least a month ahead of when I expect to transplant them into the garden. For other things—the ones I'm not growing for a prize—I start about three weeks ahead.

If I'm going to seed something into the ground, I want a good, level seedbed. For a small garden, using a rake is fine. You want it smooth, without big clods.

If your garden soil is dry, it needs water. It doesn't make any difference what temperature the water is, as long as it's not coming out in cubes! Evaporation quickly causes a cooling of the soil, but after a little bit, it comes back to normal.

Alaska soils are very new, and very infertile in the beginning. Normally, I fertilize—using a 10-20-10 or a 10-20-20—then I till the fertilizer in. For the big cabbages, I first put fertilizer and manure on the soil, and till that in, so I have lots of fertility. I do not side-dress, except when growing celery (because it is shallow rooted)

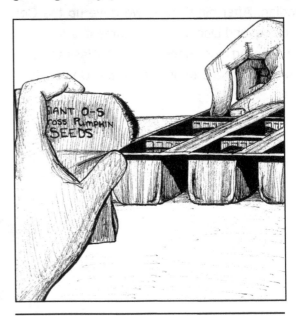

Don Dinkel plants special cabbage seeds (like O-S Cross) indoors—at least a month before he plans to transplant them into the garden—if he's planning to compete in the annual Giant Cabbage Weigh-Off at the Alaska State Fair.

and the big cabbages. I use 20-20-20 soluble fertilizer on the cabbages—every day.

Cabbage leaves spread out five feet, and so you can water them by putting PVC pipes along the ground—under the cabbages—so the water reaches the roots. Water them every-day with a couple gallons per plant.

Once the cabbages are growing, don't touch them. If you press down on them, you will start a break that continues down until you have a split cabbage that is neither marketable nor a prizewinner.

The best time to harvest your big cabbage is thirty minutes before you show them.

If you're taking them to the dinner table, shorten the time to thirty seconds. Everything is best fresh, of course.

—Don Dinkel

Till in fertilizer and manure.

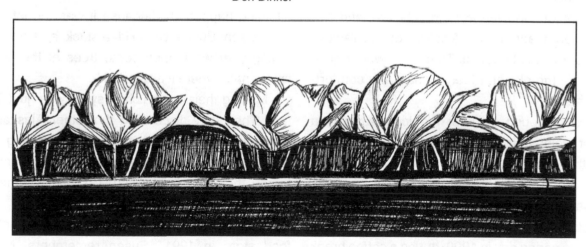

Because Alaska's soils are new, and infertile to begin with, Don first prepares his cabbage bed by applying fertilizer and manure, then tilling them in.

29 How to Make Birch Syrup

SUSAN AND DANIEL HUMPHREY, Haines
Alaskan since 1989

In 1989, Susan Humphrey, like so many women before and since, followed her husband's dream to Alaska. She and Daniel left their sunny, dry climate of New Mexico to put down new roots in the cool, moist soil of Haines, in Southeast Alaska. Within a few short years, the couple embarked on a new venture: making a variety of gourmet syrups under their own private label—Birch Boy Syrup.

The Humphreys met while attending college in New Mexico. Following graduation, married and armed with degrees in journalism and English, they headed North. Susan was expecting their first of two children.

"Daniel had lived in Haines before, and all I ever heard about was Alaska," Susan recalls. "Of course it is beautiful. There is nowhere quite like it on the planet. I feel . . . safe and comfortable here."

Daniel found work at the local sawmill, a major Haines employer at that time. After a few months, they bought their home—a renovated barn on an acre north of town. They later purchased twenty additional acres of adjoining forestland.

One spring day in 1990, during a coffee break at the mill, Daniel and his coworkers began to talk about making birch syrup. He was intrigued.

"He worked swing shift, so he came home at two-thirty in the morning, got his drill, and ran outside [to drill a hole in a birch tree]," Susan says.

The folks at Birch Boy tap the north side of their birch trees in springtime, right after they spot the first mosquito of the year. Everything must be carefully sterilized. Owner Daniel Humphrey says, "Tapping the tree is like getting a shot at the doctor's." *(Photo courtesy Daniel and Susan Humphrey)*

"Nothing happened—because it was too late in the season. But the whole idea stuck, and the following year we tapped some trees at the right time. That's where it all started."

Making their first batch of syrup was "just for fun." Then they discovered that other Alaskans were getting grant money to do the same thing on a commercial level. They learned more and soon turned their new hobby into a business named Birch Boy.

"I sold my first bottle of syrup to the health food store in 1991," Susan remembers. Now Birch Boy sells many syrup varieties, including raspberry, blueberry, elderberry, and rhubarb. But birch remains their specialty.

The Humphreys and their crew haul about 16,000 gallons of sap from the forest every spring. Each worker makes a daily circuit of about five miles to collect sap from the tapped trees.

For those who might be interested in making their own birch syrup, Susan offers one word of caution.

"We tried it the homestead way and boiled it down on our woodstove in our basement," she says. "You want to do it outside, not in your home. There's a lot of steam! People have said that they have peeled their wallpaper, or actually had their paint coming off the walls, because there are just days and days and days of boiling—with steam everywhere."

Instead, she says, use camp stoves outside. And use the widest pans you have (stainless steel only) to allow maximum surface area for evaporation, with no more than three or so inches of sap in each pan. ■

After You See the First Mosquito

YOU NEED TO TAP eight to ten trees to do this, and you will need some standard maple tree taps to keep the sap good and the trees uninfected.

Tap the trees the first week of April, or whenever you see the first mosquitoes. Tapping on the north side of our trees generally keeps the buckets in the shade longer and reduces the temperature by at least ten degrees [so] the quality of sap will last longer. Our favorite taps are made of stainless steel and are available from various maple equipment supply companies. And one thing that is very important is to sterilize everything. Tapping the tree is like getting a shot at the doctor's. We spray the general area with rubbing alcohol, and remove the dirt and lichen, but not the bark. We also sterilize the drill bit (between

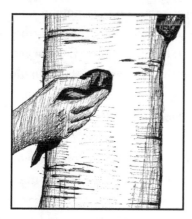

When tapping a tree, it is very important to sterilize everything. Spray the area of the tree to be tapped with rubbing alcohol and remove dirt and lichen, but not bark.

After carefully sterilizing the drill bit, drill the tap at about shoulder height on the side of the tree with the most shade. The tap itself must also be sterile.

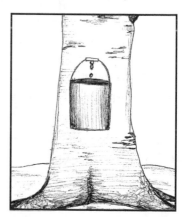

It's a good idea to tap a single tree and then wait until that tree gives about a gallon of sap per day before tapping other trees.

After You See the First Mosquito (cont'd)

each tree) and the tap itself. The buckets are washed with hot, soapy water and, sometimes, bleach. For maximum sap flow, the best place to drill the tap is at about shoulder height. We usually tap a single tree early and wait to tap others when that tree is giving about a gallon a day. You will need to boil down about 150 gallons of sap to make it worthwhile. (Plug the tap holes with small corks after you're done.)

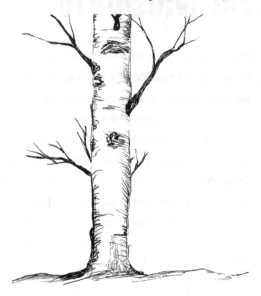

Birch syrup is very hard to make using kitchen equipment, as the sap must not be simmered for more than a half hour or so. Never mix new sap with something that has already been reduced down. That day's sap must be processed to syrup completely the same day. Also, the collection buckets must be cleaned and rinsed every day.

The best method is to bring in your ten gallons each morning, filter it through coffee filters, and place it in four three-gallon (or larger) stainless steel pots on high heat. Make sure the pans are absolutely clean, with no scorch marks. Boil as vigorously as possible but avoid scorching anywhere in the pan, including the sides. Skim off the foam. Stir and agitate to increase evaporation, until the liquid is reduced to $\frac{1}{16}$ inch, and it changes to the color of amber ale.

Watch carefully for rapid darkening, an indication that the heat is too high and that further evaporation must be at low temperatures. Another sign is bumping, a sudden eruption caused by the rapid precipitation of minerals trapping steam on the pan's surface.

Before the syrup begins to darken much, you lower the heat by transferring to double boilers. The depth of sap/syrup should be no more than $\frac{3}{8}$ inch. Any method of quickly evaporating at 200 degrees or under will work, such as a hot plate that can be regulated. In the double boilers, keep the sap moving until it resembles the thickness of hot table syrup. Remove any mineral film as it forms. Once you have only two or three ounces remaining in the pans, pour it through cheesecloth into a gallon jar, where it can decant and the sediment can settle out.

You can add to the same gallon jar each day until it is full. If you have the syrup thick enough, it will not mold or spoil even at room temperature in an unsealed bottle.

—*Susan Humphrey*

30 How to Travel with Packhorses

MARLIN GRASSER, Talkeetna, Chugach, Wrangell and Brooks
Mountain Ranges; Alaska Peninsula
Alaskan since 1947 – died September 2, 2009

Marlin Grasser was seventeen in the spring of 1947, when he first traveled to Alaska to go hunting and fishing. At the end of that summer, Marlin briefly returned to his home in Washington State and worked just long enough to earn another plane ticket to Alaska—this time for good.

"I just wanted to come back, because I felt free up here," Marlin recalled. "Back in those days, unless you robbed a bank or shot somebody, hell, nobody bothered you. The biggest share of the time, I'd take my dog and go hunting up in the hills, and if I ran out of groceries, I'd come back and get more and go out again. I had no obligations, and I really enjoyed it."

Marlin hired on that fall as an assistant hunting guide with Jack Corey, who'd come up around 1913 and lived in Chickaloon.

"Corey guided using packhorses; that's the only way you could go in those days—foot and packhorse. Didn't have airplanes to go; no snowmachines—never heard of 'em. And those awful ATVs, didn't have them either. It was by foot or horseback, and I grew up using horses."

In 1948, Marlin began working for the Jonesville coal mine, near Sutton, and continued for the following thirteen seasons.

"Each year when the mines would finish the contract, usually in May, I could either do what they called 'company work'—like timbering or cleaning up the mines—or I could take the summer off. So I chose to go hunting and fishing—for more than fifty years."

Marlin's seasonal work cycle usually consisted of mining during the winter and spring months, commercial fishing during summer, and

The late Marlin Grasser lived what was, in many ways, the Alaskan dream: He mined during the winter, commercial fished during summers, and guided hunting trips through remote areas—with the help of his pack horses—each fall. *(Photo by Nancy Gates)*

guiding hunts in the fall. A single hunt often lasted for several weeks, crossing the frigid rivers and high-mountain passes of the Talkeetna, Chugach, or Wrangell Mountains on horseback. Eventually his Alaska hunts extended north to the Brooks Range, and south to the Alaska Peninsula.

"I broke my own horses, beginning when they were three to four years old," he said. "They grew up in the mountains. I had a hundred-year grazing lease up at Boulder Creek, about thirty miles of good grazing along the river. My horses stayed up there in summer, running loose. I'd go get them for the fall hunt, and shoe them all."

When he was actively guiding, Marlin generally owned around forty packhorses and about ten to twenty colts—though at one time he had a total of eighty-five head.

To transport his packhorses to the more distant Brooks Range, Marlin would load them into a C-119 cargo plane, cross-tie them, and fly them into Arctic Village.

After fifty years of guiding with packhorses, Marlin retired from the work in 2000.

"I'm getting too old to do the shoeing and everything else that has to be done. I never hired it done, I did it all myself. I just said 'The heck with it.'"

In 2009, Marlin shared these tips on traveling with packhorses. ∎

WHEN IT COMES TO conformation, I like a short-backed, stocky horse. I like big horses, because when you swim the Copper River and the Matanuska, the bigger your horse, the longer you stay out of that water. I had quite a few horses that ran 1,500 to 1,600 pounds. A draft and thoroughbred cross makes a good-size horse, for riding and packing.

I prefer geldings to mares. You don't have a horse around all year just to look at; they all have to go to work for a couple of months a year. Geldings are more even-tempered.

Horses are by nature terrified of bears, but moose were no problem. I'd often tie a horse to the antlers of a downed moose that I was dressing out—to keep the horse from wandering off back to camp. If I had a colt that was a little leery about packing meat, I'd just take an old bloody hand and rub it all over his nose, and he'd get over it.

Borium

Having all the horseshoes hard-faced—a bead of borium welded along the edges of the shoe—enhanced traction and durability. Marlin recommended always taking extra horseshoes on a pack trip; some country has rock that is very abrasive.

Packing Horses for the Backcountry

1) Hold the folded tail of the lead horse at the base of the tailbone. Fold the free end of the second horse's lead shank to make a long loop (about 12 inches long), and lay the loop on top of the tailbone.
2) Beginning at the base of the tailbone, securely wrap the free end of the lead around the doubled tail—covering the loop, gradually working your way up the lead horse's tailbone (4 or 5 revolutions.)
3) Slip the loose end of the lead shank through the exposed loop at the top of the revolutions.
4) Pull down on the rope attached to the second horse, sliding the loop down into the revolutions and securing the free end of the lead.

I broke every horse I had to pack or ride. My horses would go through rivers or bogs and over downed trees and spooky bridges. You could mount any of them from either side. They'd go up or down any slope within reason. For really steep slopes, if possible, I'd make switchbacks to make it easier. When horses are not walking naturally, but lunging along, it's a good way to lose your pack.

I usually put a bigger horse at the front, and smaller ones toward the back. So if they're swimming and get into a bad place, that big horse will save a little horse, but a little horse couldn't pull a big one.

You have to have extra horseshoes along on a pack trip. Some country you get into has rock that is real abrasive. I had my horseshoes hard-faced with borite (borium)—a bead run all around the shoe. It made them so they didn't wear out.

I tried not to put over 200 pounds of dead weight on a horse. For multiday trips, I wouldn't put more than 150 pounds (75 pounds on a side). Equal load is very important; otherwise you can get a sore-backed horse.

You don't want weight way up high on a horse. I used regular old sawbucks and deckers (pack saddles) with breast collars and britchens. The panniers hung from saddle—right below wither height. Then I always had a top load, which wasn't heavy—sleeping bags and odds and ends—that went right on top. I'd put wooden boxes in my panniers if I wanted to protect stuff, like cakes or bread. Then you've got something to put your stove on or make cupboards out of up at the camp.

I hobbled my horses at night on the trail, and turned them loose. I'd always keep one horse in camp, and I'd ride him to go round up the others in the morning.

—Marlin Grasser

31 How to Build an Airstrip
GLEN ALSWORTH, Port Alsworth
Alaska-born in 1957

Leon "Babe" Alsworth is a well-known name in Alaska aviation history. Babe flew his own plane up to Alaska in 1939 from Minnesota before the Alaska Highway was in existence. As a commercial pilot, he flew primarily in support of the commercial fishing ventures in Bristol Bay, moving cannery workers in and out of the area.

In August 1944, Babe and his Aleut wife, Mary, homesteaded 160 acres on the shores of Lake Clark in Southcentral Alaska, land that they obtained through the agricultural Homestead Act.

Glen Alsworth takes a well-earned break from splitting firewood for his family's homestead lodge, The Farm, located at Port Alsworth in Southcentral Alaska. Son of legendary Alaska Bush pilot Babe Alsworth, Glen, and his wife, Patty, own and operate Lake Clark Air and The Farm Lodge from his family's original homestead. *(Photo courtesy Menda Fowler)*

The Alsworths met all the requirements for their homestead, which included clearing a portion of the land, planting crops, and, while living in a tent for the first year, building a cabin. Babe and Mary began constructing what became known as "the main house" in 1947 and moved into the completed house in 1952. The youngest of their five children, Glen, was born in 1954.

Like his four older brothers, Glen followed in his father's aviation footsteps and became a pilot. Today Glen is the owner and operator of Lake Clark Air, based out of the family's original homestead in a community now known as Port Alsworth.

"I began taking flying lessons in 1968 from my father," Glen recalls. "I was about fourteen years old. I got my private pilots license when I was seventeen."

Glen met his wife, Patty, when they were both attending high school in 1972. They married in 1974, and have five children—all of whom have been raised at the homestead in Port Alsworth. Like his father, Glen feeds his family on moose, caribou, and salmon, supplemented by supplies flown in from Anchorage. They also grow their own fresh produce.

"We have a large garden, in fact we call our place 'The Farm,'" Glen says. "It looks like a farm, and smells like one, too. We also have chickens, ducks, and a few pheasants . . . and we used to keep sheep, goats, and, occasionally, pigs. As neighbors moved in, we had trouble keeping the animals where they belonged, so we had to get rid of most of them."

"I don't see us moving anywhere else in the near future. Three of our five children live here in Port Alsworth, and thirteen of our twenty-three grandchildren. I wouldn't say it's impossible for us to move, the Lord can do what He wants, but I would say it seems highly improbable."

Glen has been the owner and operator of Lake Clark Air since 1977. Through his flight service and The Farm Lodge, the Alsworth family offers sightseeing, wildlife viewing, catch-and-release fishing, and photography trips within vast pieces of public land in Southwest Alaska, each designated a federal park and preserve in 1980: Lake Clark and Katmai. With more than 29,500 hours of flight experience in Alaska, Glen recalls with fondness his father's influence in his life as an aviator. But as it turns out, flying was not Babe's only passion.

"My dad was also very musical. He actually contemplated, before he settled on flying as a career, joining his brother's big band as a trumpet player. He chose flying instead, which I've been forever grateful for. A lifetime of aviation has been challenging enough, but music," he laughs, "would have been impossible!"

A significant part of the aviation challenges Glen faces on a daily basis includes maintaining the family's 100-by-3,000-foot airstrip for his Lake Clark Air business.

"We've worked our strip a lot, and it's still not enough. It's a gravel strip, and the gravel is just in its natural state, from old areas where glaciers have moved through. Unless you have a rock crusher or something, our kind of gravel is hard to compact. Of course, most times you don't have a choice—what's there is what you get, and you just have to do the best you can."

For someone considering developing a new airstrip on a remote piece of property, Glen has the following advice. ∎

Before Firing Up the Dozer . . .

THE FIRST THING I would advise anyone considering putting in an airstrip today is to check with the local land-management authority—it could be a municipality or some other type of regulatory agency—to find out what all the requirements are so you don't run afoul of the regulators. If you get crosswise with those people initially, you might not ever recover.

Choosing the right location is important. It would be ideal if the ground were flat enough to not require moving a whole lot of dirt to level things out. You'll need to clear the site of trees, most likely with a dozer.

Depending on the level of traffic, I find that grass isn't practical for an Alaska airstrip—although in some areas it does quite well. Gravel is probably one of the most stable surfaces you could have, as long as it's really gravel and not boulders. A lot of times the stones are larger, and smooth, and that's not good because the

Before Firing Up the Dozer . . . (cont'd)

stones kind of roll around and don't compact.

Also, the right orientation for wind direction is a very critical thing. I've been to some strips that were laid out without the data or knowledge of prevailing winds—and that can be a killer. A strip needs to be lined up with the winds, either straight up or down. Winds can and do blow from any direction, but there will be certain winds that will be strong enough to dictate which way you need to land. When that happens, you want your strip to be laid out so you can always land into the wind.

Typically you need some kind of wind direction indicator on your strip. If there happens to be a small pond close by, that can give you a very good wind indication; you can look at the surface of the water to see which way the wind's blowing. A wind sock or some other type of wind indicator is important.

When planning for an airstrip, it's important to first carefully consider what you hope to accomplish with it, and then build it with that idea in mind.

If you're building a private strip for, say a small, Cub-type plane, an 800- to 1,000-foot strip would be pretty good.

On the other hand, if you're building a place where you'll be bringing clients in and out, you'd probably be looking at a 2,500- to 3,000-foot strip. You might get by with a shorter strip, but you might find you won't have room for larger, more efficient aircraft.

—*Glen Alsworth*

The Alsworth family's 100-by-3,000-foot gravel airstrip supports the Lake Clark Air and The Farm Lodge businesses, and must be continually maintained.
(Photo courtesy Glen Alsworth)

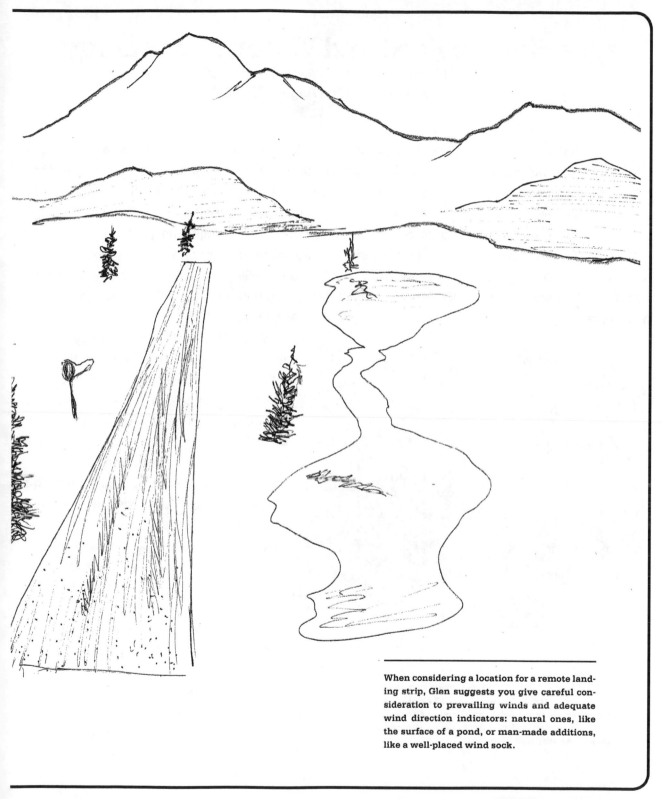

When considering a location for a remote landing strip, Glen suggests you give careful consideration to prevailing winds and adequate wind direction indicators: natural ones, like the surface of a pond, or man-made additions, like a well-placed wind sock.

32 How to Feed and Water Your Family

CLARENCE AND ANNELI BAKK, Western and Southcentral Alaska
Alaskan since 1953 - Clarence died August 22, 2011

A brief chat with Clarence Bakk about his life in Alaska will have you wondering what you've done with your own time on this earth. He, along with his wife, Anneli, taught school in seven different Alaska villages for a total of thirteen years. Clarence then taught at Alaska Bible Institute in Palmer for eighteen years, and was a commercial fisherman in Bristol Bay for forty-nine years.

The late Clarence Bakk and his wife of fifty-six years, Anneli, shared memories of their years spent teaching and raising a family in the village of Tyonek, on the northwest shore of Cook Inlet. Clarence also worked as a preacher, village medic, and commercial fisherman.
(Photo by Natalie Gates)

Born in 1926 in northern Minnesota, Clarence was the child of homesteaders on a small farm. His father was also an itinerant preacher; efficient double-tasking was an inherited trait.

Following college and a stint in the Navy, Clarence headed North to teach school at Pedro Bay, a tiny village of about fifty-five residents on Lake Iliamna—176 air miles southwest of Anchorage.

"When I first went into Pedro Bay, I drove my car to Homer, loaded with all my food, clothing, and supplies for a year. I couldn't take all the supplies with me as I flew into the village on a small charter plane, so I waited—for four months—for my supplies to come by barge across Cook Inlet."

Turns out the barge had hit a storm while crossing Cook Inlet, and all the cargo on deck had washed overboard—including Clarence's supplies. The below-deck freight was saved, but coated with mud. Clarence and another teacher from Pile Bay headed over to see what was salvageable. They dug through the mud, retrieving label-less cans that they fervently hoped contained food.

"We went back to Pedro Bay with twelve boxes of cans," Clarence recalls. "When you'd open the cans, sometimes you'd find asparagus, which I couldn't stand, and maybe the next one was a can of tar."

Sample Grocery Order from 1958

Staples:
200 lbs. flour
50 lbs. sugar
25 lbs. brown sugar
10 lbs. oatmeal
½ case Wheaties cereal
10 lbs. long spaghetti
10 lbs. elbow macaroni
25 lbs. white rice
1 case Carnation Powdered Milk
1 barrel sweet butter

Canned vegetables:
1 case whole kernel corn
1 case peas
1 case green beans
1 case whole tomatoes
½ case sweet potatoes
½ case mixed vegetables
½ case dried potato flakes

Canned meats:
1 case canned meatballs
½ case canned ham
½ case whole chickens

Dry goods:
1 case toilet paper
1 case paper towels
1 case (8 oz.) paper cups
½ case dinner napkins

That difficult first half of the school year was made easier for Clarence when a local Native family invited him to come live with them. He learned many valuable Alaska life skills during that three-month stay.

In the summer of 1954, while getting his pilot's training in Minnesota, Clarence met Anneli, his future wife, who was finishing up her degree in elementary education. They married the following summer, and three days later headed back to Alaska, this time to the village of Tyonek—on the northwest shore of Cook Inlet—where they set up housekeeping in the "teacherage."

"[It] was like an apartment—living room, kitchen, and bedroom—that was hooked onto the one main classroom," Anneli recalls, "but because we had so many students, the living room in the teacherage became my classroom."

Having been trained in the Navy Medical Corps, Clarence always became the village medic, wherever they settled. He would patch up minor injuries using basic medical supplies; for serious illnesses or injuries, he would fly the patient to an Anchorage hospital.

To feed the family, Clarence regularly hunted both moose and caribou. When successful, he hung the quarters in the family's cache behind the school—where it would freeze in wintertime. When game meat was on the menu, he would simply cut off what they needed.

As for other groceries, Anneli became used to ordering a year's worth at a time, through a company in Seattle, for barge delivery in the fall.

"Everything would come up in by the case," she says. "The first year, for example, I really didn't know how many boxes of salt there were in a case—so it was really a learning experience. I'd order canned meat, like meatballs, ham, and chicken, to supplement the moose and caribou."

Many of the groceries came packed in tins, providing rodent protection. Butter came in one-pound chunks, floating in salt water inside whiskey barrels. The Bakks stored all their groceries in the attic above the school.

Every year, the North Star supply barge made deliveries in Seward, Homer, Upper Cook Inlet (including Tyonek), then down and around the Aleutian Chain, through Bristol Bay and up Alaska's western coast. The ship made several trips from Seattle each year, but visited each coastal village only once a year. Seeing the North Star anchored in front the school was pure excitement, Clarence recalls.

"We usually closed school that day," he says, "and everybody got all their groceries for the year."

And aside from his teaching and medical chores, Clarence fetched water from a freshwater spring down at the beach, a half-mile away.

"I started carrying water everyday, as soon as school was over, usually making two trips," he remembers. "I used a wooden, shoulder yoke and two five-gallon metal Blazo cans.

"When diapers came along, the trips to the spring doubled. In the wintertime, of course, it was nearly dark by the time school was out. Sometimes I had to crawl over ten-foot icebergs that had been pushed up onto the beach."

Back inside the teacherage, the water cans were placed on the oil cookstove and warmed for cleaning and bathing. Because getting the water was so arduous, Anneli made the most of every drop, and it grew grayer with each use.

Anneli shared a sample grocery order from 1958 and offered the following tips on how to use water efficiently. ■

Good to the Last Drop

WE HAD TO BE CAREFUL in our water use. I would wash dishes and the rinse water would always be the next water for washing dishes. Then that same water might be used for washing floors or watering the garden.

It was the same with bathing the babies. I would bathe them in the sink in a little plastic dishpan. That water usually then went into a clean diaper pail or into the chemical toilet.

There was always a can for drinking water and for cooking. That stayed separate from the other water. I never had any issues about other people wasting water by washing dishes: I don't let my company wash dishes; I feel I should do it.

—*Anneli Bakk*

Anneli always made the most of every drop of water. The water used to bathe babies would then be used in the diaper pail or the chemical toilet.

Multiple trips were made every afternoon, using a wooden shoulder yoke and two five-gallon metal cans, to haul water from a stream located one-half mile away from the teacherage.

A single five-gallon can of water was always set aside for drinking and cooking purposes.

33 How to Smoke Salmon
RUSS AND FREDA ARNOLD, Ruby
Alaskan since 1956

Smoked salmon is traditional fare for Alaskans, whether it's served up on fancy platters at dinner parties in the cities, or it's hanging in the smokehouses of remote Native villages. Russ Arnold learned about smoking salmon from the experts, his Athabascan neighbors in Ruby, Alaska.

Russ is the son of dairy farmers in upstate New York. His wife, Freda, came from a family that, she says, "dabbled in farming by having a cow, a few chickens, and pigs." About five years after their marriage, in 1956, they followed a calling into missions work in the tiny Yukon River village of Ruby. By then, the couple had three children and one on the way.

In Alaska, Russ settled his family in the nearby village of Kokrines and went twenty-eight miles downriver to locate a house in Ruby. Instead he found that no housing was available, so they remained in Kokrines. A year later, a one-bedroom house was for sale.

"And it was just right for us," Russ remembers. "The house was an old one that probably was built around 1913. . . . The children slept in the bedroom; we slept out in the living room on a hide-a-bed, near the barrel stove."

With the arrival of two additional children, the Arnolds completed their family of seven. Russ kept busy, not only with his mission work, but also hauling water, cutting firewood, and putting food on the table.

Russ and Freda Arnold came to Alaska in the late 1950s to work as missionaries in the tiny Yukon River village of Ruby. Russ provided for their family—eventually numbering seven—primarily by hunting and fishing. Using a neighbor's fish wheel, Russ was able to catch abundant, delicious salmon, which they enjoyed both fresh and smoked. *(Photo by Natalie Gates)*

"While I was in Ruby, I hunted and fished to feed the family. A neighbor of mine, a Native man, had a fish wheel, and I helped him with it. When he had enough salmon for his family and their dogs, we were able to take the wheel for a little while. Once in a while I fished with a net, but I was never out there just for the fun of it. We'd get a couple of moose a year, too, and an occasional spruce grouse."

Following a hunt, Russ would first hang the moose quarters in their nearby cache to freeze, then later bring it—a quarter at a time—inside to thaw. They would cut the meat into meal-sized portions, wrap it in freezer paper, and store it either in their unheated entryway, or outside in the family Jeep for the winter. In spring, any leftover moose would be canned for summertime use.

The Arnolds had a root cellar that they made by digging through one of the existing cellar walls under the house. They ordered their staple groceries out of Anchorage once a year to be shipped up by barge and then stored in their basement. The family's ample supply of salmon was either canned by Freda, or cured in the family smokehouse.

"I bought our smokehouse from a Native man and dragged it over to our property. It was about ten feet square, and probably fifteen to eighteen feet tall. We put racks in it, and put fish on the racks up high."

In 1965, Russ founded Kokrine Hills Bible Camp, some fifty-five miles upriver from Ruby. The camp, which can only be reached by boat or by floatplane, has been a favorite place of adventure and inspiration for the children of Interior Alaska villages for more than forty years. ∎

Smokin' Good Salmon

WE USED OUR NEIGHBORS' large cutting boards that were down on a dock by the river. On one side of the floating platform was a long cutting board. On the opposite side were long, horizontal poles that we draped the fish across as we cut it.

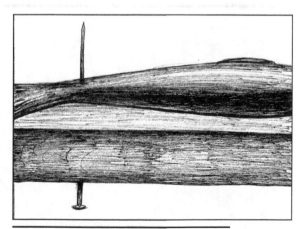

The cutting boards on the dock had a long, three-inch (tenpenny) nail driven up through one end of it. The fish tails were hammered onto the nail with a knife handles.

The cutting board had a three-inch (tenpenny) nail driven up through one end of the plank, creating a two-inch spike. We used the handle of our knives to hammer the fish tail onto the spike, with the fish lying flat on the board.

Then we inserted the knife at the tail, just in front of the nail, and with the knife held parallel to the ground, split the fish in half, lengthwise. Both halves were still connected by the tail.

We scraped the guts out, cut out the spine, and then laid out the two halves of the fish on the board, skin-side down.

We then made deep diagonal slashes, an inch or so apart, through the flesh—but not through the skin. The diagonal cuts were made in the direction that caused them to gape open when the fish was hung by the tail—to speed curing.

Smokin' Good Salmon (cont'd)

As we cut the fish, we hung them by the tails—flesh-side out—over the rods behind us on the dock.

When the rods became full, we carried them to the smokehouse and transferred the fish to the racks inside.

The floor of the smokehouse was dirt. We built the fire out of a couple two-foot-long pieces of dry cottonwood or alder, so it would smolder—not flame. We'd leave the fish in there, if we wanted to fully smoke it, for up to six weeks. All that time we'd keep the fire going.

We still love salmon, particularly kiyoga, a favorite Native salmon recipe. To make it we first soaked the salmon in brine, smoked it for about three days, and then baked it in the oven of our propane stove. It's delicious!

—*Russ and Freda Arnold*

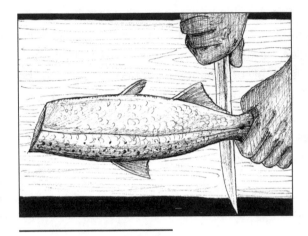

A knife is then inserted at the tail, just in front of the nail, and holding the knife parallel to the ground, split the fish in half, leaving it joined at the tail.

34 How to Assemble a First Aid Kit

ROY and MARY BETH HOOPER, Copper Center
Alaskan since 1956

Roy Hooper was twenty-three when he first came to Alaska—at the persuasive invitation of the US military. After his years in the Army, Roy worked on a farm in the Matanuska Valley, and then headed for Sheldon Jackson School in Sitka, where he served as a dorm supervisor. Mary Beth, his future wife, was a school nurse in Sitka at that time.

"Dorm supervisors had to have a first aid card, and it happened that Mary Beth taught a first aid class on my night off . . . " Roy begins. "And so the rest is history—about a fifty-year history."

Following Roy's tenure in Sitka, he and Mary Beth headed back to Southcentral Alaska and

Roy Hooper was working as a dorm supervisor at the Sheldon Jackson School in Sitka fifty-some years ago when, while fulfilling his first aid training requirement, he met first aid instructor/school nurse/future wife, Mary Beth. *(Photo by Troy Pierce)*

eventually settled in the Copper River Valley.

"I had a combine at that time, and I went out just beyond Kenny Lake to combine a field," he remembers. "I simply fell in love with that country—the beautiful mountains—and the weather was just gorgeous when I went out there."

The Hoopers both knew that they wanted to file for a homestead in the area, but Roy decided that he would first hire on with the Alaska Highway Department. They filed on their homestead land in 1961. There were three different lakes in the vicinity of the land they selected: Kenny Lake, Pippin Lake, and Willow Lake.

"They did a rectangular survey of our land, and one of the corner sections was actually in Willow Lake, so we lost some acreage. We ended up with 124 acres," Roy explains.

The Hoopers first moved a trailer out onto their homestead, built a lean-to next to it, and lived there with their growing family for almost a decade. During those years Roy cleared the land and began building their home, while continuing to work for the Highway Department.

"We had to clear twenty acres on our property and seed it with a productive crop," he says. "Unfortunately, our land was located in the lee of Willow Mountain, and areas just ten miles out from us—either to the north or south—would get almost twice the rain in summer. So we found out, after being there for two or three years, that it wasn't ideal farming country. In winter, we got about the same amount of snow as the other areas, however, because the snow came in from a different direction."

The Hoopers eventually gave up trying to farm, and Roy's job with the state sustained them. He had little interest in sportfishing, and hunted only enough to supply moose and caribou for the family. Roy's real passion was in using an adaptation of a fish wheel, which he and several of his good friends designed and built to hang from a high riverbank by a ship-styled rigging, rather than floating on a wooden dock, as ordinary fish wheels do. This allowed the men, instead of the river, to control the position of the wheel in the water, and to keep it in the best location for scooping up salmon—near the bottom of the river.

"People said it wouldn't work, but that was the most productive wheel on the river," Roy recalls with pride.

Mary Beth and a friend, along with all their children, made monthly grocery runs into Anchorage to round out their diets. Her nurse's training proved to be an invaluable skill, not only for their own family, but for many area neighbors.

"A lot of people would come to our place because they needed medical help and we had one of the few telephones around," Roy says. "Mary Beth would either patch them up—using medical supplies she always kept on hand—and send them along, or else she'd call the Cross Road Medical Center, which is located roughly thirty miles to the north in Glennallen—and tell them that a patient was headed their way."

These days, health reasons have compelled the Hoopers to live closer to the city. But their original home, built by Roy in those early years, is now owned and occupied by their son and daughter-in-law.

Roy and Mary Beth offered the following suggestions for assembling a dependable first aid kit. The late Dr. Charles Manwiller, another longtime Alaskan who was in family practice in Anchorage for more than fifty years, also contributed to the list. ■

The Hoopers soon moved to homestead in the beautiful Copper River Valley, where they raised their family. *(Photo courtesy Roy Hooper)*

Building a First Aid Kit

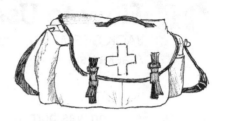

FIRST AID KITS MAY BE stored in a variety of different containers. One good option would be a sturdy, waterproof, wide-mouth duffle with a variety of pockets. Every first aid kit should include a reliable first aid manual. (Dr. Manwiller recommended: *Mountaineering First Aid*, 5th edition, Jan D. Carline, Martha J. Lentz, and Steven C. MacDonald.)

A sturdy, waterproof, wide-mouth duffel allows easy access to first aide supplies when emergency situations arise. A concise, reliable first aid manual is essential, as well.

Antiseptic solution
Antibiotic ointment
Soap, or hand-
    sanitizer
Sterile eyewash solu-
    tion, like saline
Instant cold packs
Tweezers
Scissors
Sewing needle
Safety pins
Thermometer
Aluminum finger splints
Adhesive tape

Elastic wrap (such as
    Ace™ bandages)
Triangular bandages
Butterfly bandages
Steri-strips, ¼-inch and
    ½-inch widths
Bandage strips
    (like Band-Aids®, Curads®—
    in a variety of sizes)
Cotton balls
Cotton swabs
Latex (or non-latex) gloves
Hydrocortisone cream
    (over-the-counter)
Aspirin (never give to children)
Nonaspirin pain re-
    liever (Tylenol®)

Ibuprofen
Calamine lotion
Antidiarrheal
    medication (like
    OTC Imodium®)
EpiPen® (auto-injector of epi-
    nephrine for allergic attacks)
Syringe
Medicine cup
Spoon
Emergency numbers (doctor,
    hospital, poison control)
Satellite phone, or cell
    phone and charger
    that plugs into car
Flashlight, with extra batteries
Candles
Matches
Mylar emergency blankets
   —*Roy and Mary Beth Hooper*

People in very remote areas need to have adequate first aid supplies on hand, and a plan for how and when to use them. Mary Beth's nursing training was an invaluable asset to their family, as well as their neighbors.

How to Use Horsepower to Haul Wood

JACK SEEMANN, Lazy Mountain
Alaskan since 1949

John "Jack" Seemann was born in Chicago in January 1931, into a rich family legacy of love and self-sufficiency. Jack learned from his parents and grandparents the carpentry and farming skills—as well as a devotion to country life—that prepared him for his adventurous future in Alaska. He also inherited a tenacious (some might call it stubborn), can-do mind-set that has proven invaluable over the years.

It was a combination of the stories Jack heard from a family friend who had spent his war years in Alaska, the Jack London tales he loved to read, and the wanderlust he inherited from his maternal grandfather (a ship's carpenter from Scotland) that drew Jack to Alaska in June of 1949. Encouraged by his parents to go check it out for himself, he purchased a one-way ticket on Northwest Airlines and headed north—with $90 in his pocket.

Jack quickly found work, first on the slimeline of a Valdez cannery and later as a section hand, or "gandy dancer," for the Alaska Railroad. Jack spent many of his free weekends helping friends clear their 160 acres of land on Lazy Mountain, northeast of Palmer.

In 1951, he became a telephone lineman for the railroad, but his career was soon interrupted by a two-year military commitment in Korea. In February 1954, he headed back to Alaska.

"When I got back I found that there were no

Much of Jack's original farmland was cleared using "horse-power" instead of today's dozers and tractors. Here he is with one of his mares, Gracie, and her new colt, Blue. *(Photo by Nancy Gates)*

railroad jobs for a lineman, and I didn't want to go back to being a gandy dancer, so I thought I'd try my hand at farming in the Matanuska Valley," he remembers.

Jack withdrew his railroad retirement money, almost $500, and bought 140 acres on Lazy Mountain—at $5 an acre. When spring came, he moved onto his new land, lived in a tent, and began logging for his cabin. He named his farm Pitchfork Ranch.

Jack's inherited tenacity paid off as he soon completed his cabin, found work on a maintenance crew for the farmers' cooperative, and learned many vital farming skills from neighboring homesteaders. With their helpful advice, and the use of some of their equipment, Jack began to clear his land.

In 1955, Jack enlarged his farm by buying an additional 200 acres of land from the government. Three years later, he married Jane Pettit, a neighbor and good friend who had lost her first husband to cancer the previous winter. With Jane's and her three children's help, Jack finished work on his barn, and began a thirty-by-twenty-four-foot addition to the cabin.

"It was a happy time. We really worked hard, the kids pitched right in and we became a family I was proud of."

Over the years, Pitchfork has been home, not only to Jack and his family, but also to a variety of livestock. Favorite among them are Jack's beloved Percheron horses: giant, hearty draft horses who, like Jack, are known for their good sense and reliable work ethic.

In the early 1970s, Jack purchased an additional 150 acres of land adjoining his farm. While much of the clearing was done with dozers and tractors, Jack enjoys working with his horses in the coldest months. ■

Jack Seemann first arrived in Alaska in 1949. After working at a Valdez cannery, then later as a "gandy dancer" for the Alaska Railroad, Jack eventually decided to try his hand at farming in the beautiful Matanuska Valley. *(Photo by Nancy Gates)*

Horses That Count

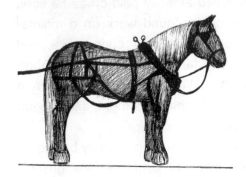

I USUALLY LOG OR HAUL firewood with the horses during winter, because I'm too busy with other things in the summer.

Before we start logging, we have to put some new ice shoes on the horses to keep them from slipping and falling.

I hitch two horses up to my bobsled. I fell the trees so they are parallel to the slope of the hill, then I bring the sled up alongside and roll the logs onto the sled.

When hauling logs, I generally load the sled with two 24-footers, then about three 12-footers, and then a couple of 10-footers on top.

On the steep spot of the trail, I drag a log behind the sled to act as a brake. It works well. Sometimes I sprinkle five gallons of ashes along one of the sled tracks on the way up the hill, and that gives a better grip on the way down.

If it's firewood I'm bringing in, I first put 12-inch wooden side rails on the sled, then load it

Jack enjoys hitching up his Percheron draft horses to haul wood during the winter. He first puts ice shoes on the horses to keep them from slipping and falling.

with about 170 pieces of firewood. And those horses can count! When I get around 160 pieces of wood loaded, they start pulling into the collars. They didn't agree with my count once, and they went all the way home without me.

It's good if your horses respond to voice commands, so if they decide you've loaded enough firewood, you can yell "Whoa!" and stop them. Then you get to ride home on the sled, rather than walk.

—*Jack Seemann*

Jack generally loads his bobsled with two 24-foot logs, then about three 12-footers, then a couple of 10-footers on top.

36 How to Tie Useful Knots
STEVE AXELSON, Ketchikan
Alaska-born in 1963

Steve Axelson stays busy doing what his father, his uncles, his grandfather, and possibly even his great-grandfather did before him: commercial fishing in Southeast Alaska.

"I know that my grandfather and my great-uncles fished every summer in the Gulf of Alaska," Steve says. "My father earned his money for college by fishing, and then became a banker. But his brothers were all fishermen. So I'm at

Like his father and grandfather before him, Steve Axelson makes his living from Alaska's oceans. Having owned and operated cannery tenders for nearly twenty years, Steve now hires skippers to continue running the tenders while he trains to become a marine pilot. *(Photo courtesy Steve Axelson)*

Commercial fishing has always been a family effort for the Axelsons. Here, (son) Paul Axelson is busy pumping herring. *(Photo courtesy Steve Axelson)*

least the third generation of Axelsons making a living on Alaska waters."

Steve earned his own way through college by working aboard various types of commercial fishing vessels.

"I was on two or three different seiners," he remembers. "I've gillnetted, and I worked on my uncle's cannery tender out of Haines for several seasons."

Not long after graduating from college, Steve was contacted by Excursion Inlet, a cannery located about six hours (by boat) from Juneau.

The cannery needed an additional fish tender, and they knew Steve was available. Knowing that the cannery work was a certainty, Steve bought his first tender in 1993.

"As a tender owner, I work for several different canneries or cold storages. They usually give me their checkbook, and I head out to the fishing grounds. I go alongside each commercial fishing boat and off-load their catch onto my boat," Steve says.

"My boat is quite a bit larger than a fishing boat; I can service maybe twenty fishing boats in one trip. I write the fishermen a check for the amount of their catch. Then the fishing boats can stay out and keep fishing, and I can bring a fresh product into town."

Knots play many vital roles aboard commercial fishing vessels, even in mundane chores like drying laundry. Here's what wash day looks like aboard *Champion*. *(Photo courtesy Steve Axelson)*

After purchasing his tender, Steve needed to hire his crew. On the advice of his father, he hired a twenty-one-year-old woman, Nancy, whose family attended his church. She and Steve made a good team, and about a year later they married. They worked together on the boat for two years, until they started their family. Today the Axelsons have six children. Steve eventually purchased a second boat, though his work on the tenders meant long absences from the family.

"I actually worked, at first, out of Excursion Inlet, Icy Straight, and Lynn Canal. I would spend about 100 days each summer in the waters of the northern part of Southeast and wouldn't return home to Ketchikan at all during that time."

In 2003, Steve was able to begin to work out of Ketchikan, allowing him to come home two or three times each week, and making life easier for the whole family. Still, it is strenuous work, with an uncertain future, in Steve's opinion.

"My tender days are slowly waning for me. I keep getting older, even though my deck hands stay college-aged. Also, since the advent of farmed fish, my income and the number of days with the cannery tender were declining and I didn't see any future in it. I was ready for a change."

So for the past couple of years, Steve has been in training to become a marine pilot for the Southeast Alaska Pilots Association—a four-year endeavor. As a pilot he will board cargo and cruise ship vessels and guide them safely through the Inside Passage. While he has been in the training program, Steve has hired skippers to continue running his two tenders.

"They're actually supporting my pilotage habit right now, and I'll have at least a couple more years of fishing, no matter what. I still go out on the boats in wintertime for the crab and herring fisheries. I occasionally tend or even fish for King crab, but only between Petersburg and Juneau in Southeast—so it's not like *The Deadliest Catch*."

Steve has learned many valuable skills during his years of commercial fishing. One that he always passes on to crewmembers is how to tie reliable knots—an important skill on land or sea. ■

Work aboard Steve Axelson's two cannery tenders has meant long absences from his family during fishing season. That, plus the financial blow dealt the industry by farmed fishing, have prompted Steve to work toward becoming a marine pilot. *(Photo courtesy Steve Axelson)*

Knots to Know

WE'RE USING KNOTS every day on a fishing boat, whether we're lashing something down, pulling something along, or hanging things on rails for storage. Most of the knots you use on a boat, you could for many other purposes.

There are lots of knots that people use that you can't untie. Since on a boat we're constantly using the same lines for different situations, I teach all my deckhands the same basic knots.

We frequently have to adjust the height of the buoy bags that hang from the rails of the boat, and we have a common knot that makes that adjustment much easier: a clove hitch. We also use a clove hitch if we have a coil of line we want to get up off the deck. We'll use a smaller piece of line and tie the coil up to a handrail. We usually follow clove hitch with a half hitch. We use that combination all the time. You can tie this knot when there's tension on the line.

Sometimes you need a knot at the end to increase the diameter of the line. We either use

Knots to Know (cont'd)

an overhand knot for that—or a figure eight. You can get a figure-eight knot undone—that's the nice thing about it, they don't get too tight. I call that kind of knot in the end of a line a stopper.

A common knot we use to tie a loop in the end of a line is called the bowline. You can also get a bowline undone, no matter how much tension has been on it.

We also splice eyes at the end of lines. Eye splices are like having a permanent bowline on the end of your line. You make a loop, and then weave the end of the rope back into itself. A spliced rope will retain about 80 percent of the rope's tensile strength; a knot crimps the fibers of the rope, and will always result in a weaker line than a spliced rope.

—*Steve Axelson*

Half Hitch

Figure Eight

Bowline Knot

Clove Hitch

Eye Splice Knot

37 How to Avoid—or Survive— Falling Through the Ice

BOB UHL, Kotzebue
Alaskan since 1945

Bob Uhl was eighteen at the end of World War II, in 1945 when the Army brought him to Alaska. He was assigned to a remnant of the 1st Combat Intelligence Platoon, better known today as Castner's Cutthroats, a colorful cadre of hunters, trappers, miners, and Native Alaskans who were uniquely adept at surviving the elements while carrying out daring missions—namely, retaking land occupied by the Japanese in the Aleutians.

Just prior to the end of his military service, Bob's unit was assigned to the Army's Arctic Indoctrination School, where they were tasked with teaching Arctic survival skills to incoming Air Force and Army aviation personnel.

"The idea was for those folks to come to Kotzebue, spend the first night in a ready-made snow house out on the ice. Then the next day they would be required to make their own snow house, then spend the second night there. The third day, if they survived that, they went back to their station."

While stationed in Kotzebue, Bob met his future wife, Carrie, at the local movie hall.

"Her folks, the Eskimo folks here in the Kotzebue area, were—and continue to be—somewhat nomadic," he says. "They moved around in a yearly cycle to those places that provided something you catch, something to eat, something to live on. Her parents had raised ten kids just living off the land in the old manner, and that was pretty

Bob Uhl has accumulated considerable wisdom about life in the Arctic over the past sixty-seven years. It began with his Arctic military training as a member of Castner's Cutthroats, and was then enhanced by his many years of living with his wife, Carrie, an Iñupiat Eskimo and her nomadic family. *(Photo courtesy Seth Kantner)*

attractive to me, a California kid who—particularly after the atom bombs were dropped—didn't feel like he had much of a future to look forward to. I had a great urge to learn how to live off the land."

Bob fulfilled his military commitment in 1948, and married Carrie. As a couple, they joined in her family's traditional lifestyle, which changed with the seasons. They spent the months from late April to early July on a gravel beach called Sisualik, then headed down the coast to catch whitefish until freeze-up.

"They'd put up as much fish as they could for a winter food source," Bob remembers. "Then, in November, there would be another move back into a timber patch where you could find enough wood through the coldest part of the winter, to keep yourself from freezing to death."

The Army, inadvertently, had begun Bob's training by placing him with men already savvy in Arctic life skills. Carrie's family then completed his education as they graciously absorbed him into the family's nomadic lifestyle.

"It was not real hard for me to mimic the things they knew—and thereby surviving to the ripe old age of eighty-four," Bob says.

Among the many skills he learned was how to carefully navigate ice. ■

IF YOU ARE TRYING TO gather natural resources that live out on the ice, you're always taking chances of one kind or another. Inevitably, you can fall through the ice at any time.

But there are different kinds of ice. Saltwater ice, where you spend a lot of time out in the ocean, is very elastic—even though it waves up and down when you walk on it. Freshwater ice is brittle: it doesn't wave up and down; it just breaks and you fall through.

If you use the tools of the people who live on the ice, you'll have your *aiyauppiaq*, a wooden pole with a metal tip, testing every step you

Bob Uhl says that people who live on the ice always have a long wooden pole with a metal tip, an *aiyauppiaq*, with them to test every step they take. Dark-colored snow patches are suspect, and must be first poked with the *aiyauppiaq* to test for strength before stepping there.

Tools for Survival

take. Unconsciously, you just put it down as you are walking along, whether on thick or thin ice. It's like your right arm, or a second hand; you don't feel comfortable unless you have it.

Any dark-colored snow patches are suspect right away. If you can't, or don't want to go around it, you poke the dark place with your *aiyauppiaq*—to see how strong it is.

Thin places in freshwater ice are usually caused by the current underneath. That becomes a very deadly problem. It's hard to notice the thin place before you fall through—especially if fresh snow is falling.

Saltwater ice is usually current-free and a lot friendlier than freshwater ice. If saltwater ice is thin, it tends to melt any new-fallen snow rather quickly, soon making a dangerous place darker—even during a snowstorm.

If you misjudge the strength and fall through the ice, hopefully you're not empty-handed. You have to have some way to distribute your weight when you are trying to crawl out. The *aiyauppiaq* is wide enough to help.

Another important tool is the knife on your belt. You reach out as far as you can reach and chip

If you misjudge the ice and fall through, your *aiyauppiaq* will help distribute your weight as you try to crawl out. You can also use your knife to reach out as far as possible, chip out a hole in the ice, then jab the knife into the hole to try and leverage yourself out of the water.

the ice. Then jab the knife into the hole you've made and use it to leverage yourself out of the hole. It may not take all of your weight, but it would take a considerable amount and allow you to drag the rest of your body out onto the ice.

Stay flat on the ice as you slide away from the hole. Get rid of wet clothes and use anything at hand to dry off. You might build a fire or climb into a sleeping bag. You can utilize the dependable heat of a running snowmachine, being careful not to asphyxiate or burn yourself. If you've got a dog team handy, it's easier to share their warmth.

—Bob Uhl

38 How to Can Salmon on the Beach

DOLORES STEFFES, Knik River
Alaskan since 1957

Plain curiosity drove the Steffes family to Alaska in September 1957. George and Dolores, traveling with their two preschoolers and a baby, drove up the Alaska Highway from Minnesota. The folks back home thought they were crazy.

"We just wanted to see what color the grass was up here—to have an adventure," Dolores recalls. "George was driving ahead of me—with the middle daughter—in a 1949 Dodge panel, and other girls and I followed him in a 1954 Dodge sedan."

In 1962, George and Dolores Steffes built this prove-up cabin on their 160-acre homestead in the Knik River area. "Our cabin was the first permanent dwelling in this valley," says Dolores. "We were the original homesteaders." *(Photo by Nancy Gates)*

Now an eighty-one-year-old widow, Dolores retains the strong, lean carriage of her pioneering past. Her deadpan, no-nonsense expression does not successfully hide her keen wit and hospitable heart.

"Now our family doesn't think we're crazy anymore. They know it," she declares, straight-faced.

Shortly after their arrival in Anchorage, the couple purchased two small home sites in North Birchwood. Five years later, after proving up on the property, George and Dolores subdivided and sold the land, then started over—with new raw land, a 160-acre homestead in the Knik River area.

"Out here, on the homestead, the rules were different," Dolores remembers. "You had to cultivate $\frac{1}{16}$ or $\frac{1}{20}$ of the land—I'm not sure. And you had to build a cabin. Our prove-up cabin was the first permanent dwelling in this valley; we were the original homesteaders."

After the cabin was up, Dolores and the children moved to the homestead while George split his time between home and North Birchwood, where he worked construction. The girls—at that time almost eight, ten, and twelve years old—worked hard as most homestead children do. But they also played hard, and handled their schoolwork by mail.

"I was out here for three winters, just the kids and me," Dolores says. "We had everything we needed: a couple of cows, a couple of pigs, a goat, and rabbits. I did the sawing of wood with the chain saw. The girls had the hard work of hauling the wood in and splitting it.

"We had a lot to do," she adds, "but we had a lot of fun, too. The kids loved life on the homestead, and they especially loved to read. They spent many hours curled up with books. They even designed a little theater, out among the spruce trees, where they would act out Shakespeare's plays for an adoring audience of one or two. They were really good! We played all kinds of board games and card games at the kitchen table in the evenings; we still do. I enjoyed it, homesteading. I'd do it again today, if I could."

The Steffes family enjoyed their life of self-sufficiency. They lived on vegetables grown in their garden, livestock they raised on the homestead, and the area's wild game and salmon—all of which had to be preserved for use over long Alaska winters.

"We didn't have a root cellar. We had a great, big, wooden box, not quite as wide as this kitchen table, but about the same length and height. It sat outside the door of the cabin. So when I canned food, and waited until the jars were cool enough that the outside cold air wouldn't break them, I'd put them out there in that box. Over the years, I don't think I lost more than two jars from freezing and breaking."

Dolores Steffes fondly recalls her homesteading years. The family enjoyed a life of self-suffi-ciency: eating vegetables from their garden, meat from livestock they raised, and wild game and salmon—all of which had to be harvested and preserved for the long winters. *(Photo by Nancy Gates)*

Each summer, Dolores and a neighbor—a local Native woman—would take their combined total of ten children out on an extended salmon fishing trip at a Goose Bay set net site.

"We had a ninety-foot long by twelve-foot deep net. The men wouldn't let us take the boat out to tend the net—which would have been a lot easier—because of the dangerous tides. So we had to wait until the tide went out, and the net laid on the mud flats. Then we'd either walk out on top of the net, or we used bear-paw snowshoes so we wouldn't get stuck in the mud. We'd pick the fish out of the net, clean them, and can them right on the beach." ∎

Oceanside Canning

TAKE ALONG SEVERAL CASES of clean, wide-mouth, pint canning jars. You do not have to sterilize them when you cold pack.

Get a clean, fifteen-gallon oil drum, and put something—like wire—on the bottom of it, because the jars can't sit directly on the bottom of the pan.

You don't scale the salmon. You just clean it, cut it up, and put it—bones, skin, and all—into the canning jars, along with about a half teaspoon of salt and no liquid. The fish will make its own liquid (and so will meat).

Then put the lids on, hand tighten, and then loosen them just a little bit.

Then, just stack the jars inside the drum as high as you can, cover them with water, and put the drum on a Coleman-style camp stove. Bring the water to a boil for about four hours. Then take the jars out, let them cool, and that's it.

You can any meat the same way . . . moose, bear, yak, caribou, chicken, or tur-

To can salmon on the beach, Dolores recommends you take along several cases of clean, though not necessarily sterilized, pint canning jars.

key. When company shows up, you can simply open a can of meat, make some gravy, and it's like having fast food! It will keep forever, as long as the seal doesn't break.

Frozen meat, on the other hand, will eventually get freezer burned or spoil if the electricity goes out.

[Editor's note: To be absolutely certain that you are following safe canning practices, please contact your local Cooperative Extension Service for their recommendations for safely canning salmon and other foods.]

—*Dolores Steffes*

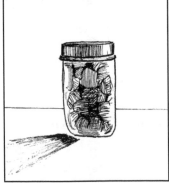

Clean the salmon, cut it up into chunks, and put it—bones, skin, and all—into the canning jars and add about a half teaspoon of salt.

Next, put the lids onto the jars, hand tighten, then loosen "just a little bit."

39 How to Build a Raised-Bed Garden
CHARLOTTE JEWELL, Skagway
Alaskan since 1974

Henry Clark, the "Rhubarb King," was a major player in Skagway during the gold rush era of the late 1890s. He sold fresh produce, including rhubarb of legendary size, to thousands of miners pouring through Skagway en route to the Klondike, successfully farming a forty-acre parcel west of the Skagway River Bridge.

Today, a portion of Clark's original farm is under cultivation by another well-known local farmer, Charlotte Jewell. But instead of growing food for miners headed over the White Pass or Chilkoot Trail, she's growing show gardens, giving visitors a chance to see the abundance of vegetables and flowers that flourish under the Midnight Sun.

Charlotte was not new to agriculture when she came to Alaska in 1974. Her father was a dairy farmer in Pennsylvania, and her mother—and grandmothers—were gardeners.

"Both my grandmothers were born and raised in England, and I think if you've got British ancestry, you've got a little bit of sap in your blood," she jokes.

Charlotte Jewell was not new to gardening when she moved to Alaska in 1974. Her mother and grandmother before her were both gardeners. But she learned about Alaska gardening techniques, like raised beds, through trial and error and by consulting the Cooperative Extension Service. *(Photo courtesy Charlotte Jewell)*

Charlotte's college degree is in art history, but the majority of her classes centered on the art side of the equation—studio work. She credits Alaska's pipeline boom with her decision to venture North.

"My brother had spent some time up here. He had a bit of the wanderlust, and traveled all over North America, from Panama up. He came up to Alaska a couple of years before I did, and it kind of fired up my own desire for adventure."

So Charlotte loaded up her car. She soon found work, first in Anchorage and later in Skagway, creating bone and ivory carvings. In 1978, she met her future husband, James Jewell, a National Park Service employee in Skagway. They have one son, Max. Charlotte owned a gift shop in Skagway when Max was born, and continued to operate it for a few more years, until gardening grew more distracting.

"I discovered that Skagway was once known as the 'Garden City of Alaska,'" she says. "In fact, as early as 1902, the town had its first garden competition. That information really piqued my interest; it just seemed like that was something Skagway should promote. I wanted to give the town a big, successful garden."

So Charlotte sold her business and began searching for land. She found one interesting parcel that was about 1½ acres and held a piece of Skagway history: the original home site of Henry Clark's farm. The city owned the land, and while they were not interested in selling, they did grant Charlotte a long-term lease. Eventually, she was able to acquire another three-plus acres adjoining her leased land. An acre of her garden is on city property.

"The town of Skagway is a pretty small site—basically the flood plain of a river. Most of the soil is very rocky," Charlotte says. "The area of Clark's home site, I suspect, was a sandbar, because the soil was very sandy, and I think that's why Henry Clark set up there. He died in 1945, and for fifty-one years the land sat there. It was a field where locals grazed their livestock or camped. Fortunately, because Clark had worked it, the soil was pretty good."

In fall 1996, Charlotte bought a Bobcat and began to implement her dream of creating "Jewell Gardens," an Alaska show garden of both flowers and organic vegetables. In addition to touring the gardens, visitors can enjoy lunch, sip afternoon tea, or even try their hand at glassblowing.

Charlotte Jewell says she learned about gardening—not only from her mother and grandmothers—but also through trial and error, and by consulting the Cooperative Extension Service. ■

Gardening in Zone 6a

RAISING THE BED ALWAYS raises the soil temperature. You have the advantage of warmer soil earlier in the season. It extends your season by a month in each direction, easily.

It's best to make a wooden raised bed, but even just raised soil is better than nothing.

I've used old railroad ties and put old glass windows on top to make a crude raised bed.

Normally, I use 2-by-12-by-16 rough-cut lumber, so the bed measures 12 inches high, 16 feet long, and 3 feet wide. If made much wider, it's hard to reach to the center.

Having a raised bed is great as you get older. You can make a place to sit by adding a 2-by-6 flat ledge around the top.

To further extend the season, you cover the bed with Visqueen-style plastic sheeting. Support the plastic with a series of arches made from flexible plastic tubing. I just push the plastic pipe into the soil on the inside of the wood. You can buy brackets like those used to attach conduit.

Then I cut a piece of Visqueen to the appropriate size to cover the bed. I then take two 2-by-4-by-16 boards, staple the long edges of the sheeting to them, roll them up like a scroll, and then place them over the plastic tubing, unrolling enough so that the boards rest on the ground and the bed is covered. If I want to open the bed during the day, I just roll the plastic sheeting up.

I cap the ends of the beds by driving two posts into the ground at each end, then stapling inexpensive, rigid corrugated plastic—that I cut using a sharp utility knife—to the posts.

—Charlotte Jewell

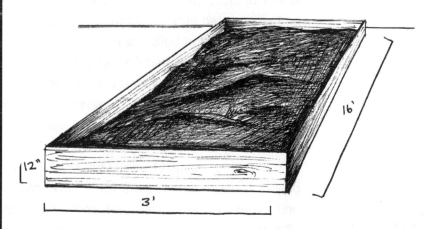

Charlotte builds her raised beds from 2-by-12-by-16 foot rough-cut lumber. The finished bed dimensions are 12 inches high, 16 feet long, and 3 feet wide, making it easy to reach the center of the beds. A 2-by-6 flat ledge added around the top of the frame would provide a comfortable place for the gardener to sit.

40 How to Overwinter Chickens

GLORIA DAY, Valdez
Alaskan since 1945

The Day family at Valdez about 1955 : (back row) Walter, Gloria, Linda, Bob, and Sandy; (front row) Patrick (with his puppy) and Wanda. *(Photo courtesy Gloria Day)*

The new young clerk at Gilson's Grocery that fall of 1945 was named Gloria. She was twenty-three years old, had just moved up from Columbus, Ohio, and had not worked at Gilson's for more than two weeks when Walter Day strolled into the store and struck up a conversation with the new girl in town.

"He asked me what I had done before I came up here," Gloria recalls. "I said I was a bookkeeper for a landholding company in Columbus, and that I handled billing for them. So Walt must have gone home and told his dad. The Day family had a salmon cannery across the bay, Dayville Packing Company. So Andrew Day, Walt's dad, came over and offered me a job as bookkeeper. The wages weren't too good, but they included a

Gloria holding "Loti," her companion and playmate in the front yard of her home in Valdez in 2007. *(Photo courtesy Linda Day Guthrie)*

place to live—and, of course, Walt was pretty good-looking in those days."

In 1900, the Army established Fort Liscum on the shores of Port Valdez. Charged with maintaining law and order during the gold rush days as well as building a military road and telegraph line to Interior Alaska, the fort completed its work and was closed in 1923. Andrew and Oma Bell Day bought the fort buildings in 1929.

"The military still had control of the land, but the Day family homesteaded over the top of the military holding—with the understanding that when the Army released the property, they would get it. And that's how Dayville came to be."

On that fall day in Gilson's Grocery, Walt had only recently returned home from the Army. He and Gloria began to "see one another" shortly after their casual conversation and, in January, they decided to get married.

Throughout their fifty-five years of marriage, Gloria and Walt wore a number of different hats. They were licensed pilots, real estate brokers, and insurance agents. Together they worked in the family cannery business, owned a clothing store, started a newspaper, commercial fished, owned a dairy farm (in Ohio), participated in numerous rescue operations through the Coast Guard Auxiliary, and ran a sawmill, restaurant, service station, and garage.

In their spare time they proved up on their own homestead—six miles outside of Valdez—and raised five children. Gloria also worked as a bookkeeper, payroll clerk, and following the 1964 earthquake, postmaster. Among their many economic enterprises was a season of raising chickens.

"The only eggs you could get up here were boat eggs—eggs shipped by boat—and they were not what you'd call fresh. We thought raising chickens would be a good thing to do; it would bring us income in the winter when the cannery was put to rest."

In the following, Gloria recalls, with good humor, the lessons learned from that particular endeavor. ■

Keeping Chickens Warm

As usual, we dove in with both feet. We got the chickens when we were living at Dayville in the late 1940s.

First, Walt built the chicken house—a large, flat-roofed structure with roosts placed at one end of the house, and nesting boxes at the opposite end. He put a boiler with pipes running through the floor to heat it. For bedding we used wood shavings or sawdust.

We had our own power plant over there, powered by water. So in the summertime we had plenty of power—but not so much in winter. We did manage to put a few lights in the chicken house in winter.

We ordered our feed up from an outfit in Washington, and it came up by boat. Then we got 2,000 baby leghorn chicks. We chose leghorns because they were good layers.

The chickens ran loose inside the chicken

If you keep your chickens in an outdoor coop during the warmer months, it's important to protect them from predators, like foxes, that dig under the fence, as well as falcons or ravens, who fly into the enclosure. Wrapping the fencing underneath the coop will help thwart diggers, and covering the top with some type of fencing material, or even strands of barbed wire crisscrossed overhead, will discourage airborne enemies.

house, which was ventilated in summer and closed up in winter.

We found out that 2,000 chickens generate so much heat that you don't need a boiler or

Keeping Chickens Warm (cont'd)

pipes in the floor for added warmth. The boiler was never fired up, after all that work of putting it in.

In fact, the flock generated so much heat that, as moist as it is down here, we had a problem. The ceiling would actually drip during the wintertime; it would "rain" on the chickens.

We sold eggs in Valdez and up the highway as far as Palmer. We had some people say, "These eggs don't have any taste!" That was because they were used to the flavor of old boat eggs.

We kept chickens for a couple of years, and then the cost of shipping feed up here became prohibitive. So we decided to get out of the chicken business.

We sold fryers all up and down the highway. We had to butcher and clean all those chickens, and that was quite a job.

—*Gloria Day*

To successfully overwinter a small flock of chickens in Alaska, Darlene DeVilbiss recommends:

- A well-insulated chicken house with roosts (approximately one inch in diameter to allow the chickens a good grasp) stair-stepped up on the far end of the house. Each roosting pole should be at least twelve inches above and beyond the previous one.
- A timer connected to a lightbulb overhead provides the necessary twelve hours of light, followed by twelve hours of darkness.
- Hay bales stacked around the base of the chicken house add insulation against bitter cold days and nights.
- Adequate food and fresh water must be provided throughout the day. Darlene finds that in her eight-by-eight foot chicken house, housing around twenty-five chickens will usually generate enough heat to keep the chickens' water thawed.

- Nesting boxes must be provided—one for every three or four hens.
- Wood shavings work well for bedding. Keep adding layers throughout the winter. The covered manure helps generate heat.

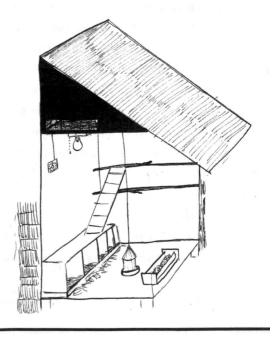

41 How to Spin Dog Fur

CHARILYN CARDWELL, Palmer
Alaskan since 1972

Charilyn Cardwell knows a thing or two about fibers, and not just ordinary fibers. Exotic ones. After learning to knit at the tender age of six in East Wenatchee, Washington, she later honed her fiber skills as a teenager, with the kind assistance of a lady in a nearby knit shop. Charilyn sold her first hand-knitted sweater before she graduated from high school.

In 1969, Charilyn graduated from college and married her sweetheart, Bob—a man with the portentous last name of Cardwell. For the first three years of their marriage, the couple taught school in Washington, then ventured to Alaska to teach for two years in the tiny Southeast community of Kake. They invested the balance of their teaching careers in the sprawling Matanuska Valley of Southcentral—where they still reside today.

Retired from teaching, Charilyn operates her own fiber business, Woofer Wearables. She happily fills her days spinning yarns and knitting hats, gloves, scarves, sweaters, and other commissioned projects—primarily from dog fur and other exotic fibers.

"I'd always liked fuzzy animals for some reason," she remembers, "and I'd always wanted an Old English Sheepdog. So we when we rented a house out in the Butte [near Palmer], we got one. He was a show dog and, of course, they take daily brushings, I thought, 'Surely I can do something with all this fiber. I'm going to take a class and learn to spin.'"

So in the early 1980s, Charilyn took a spinning course at Mat-Su Community College, specifically to learn how to spin dog fur.

"I'd already decided that," she says. "I never cared about wool. I liked all the exotic fibers."

Charilyn has even spun fiber from the camels in the Anchorage Zoo (sometimes blended with alpacas or sheep fiber) and sells it and other knitted items as a fund-raising effort for the zoo. Her products can be found in the zoo's gift shop, the Anchorage Museum shop, and at a local yarn shop.

Retired schoolteacher Charilyn Cardwell operates her own unique fiber business. Here she displays a beautiful, warm mitten spun from yarn made of dog fur. *(Photo by Nancy Gates)*

While her fiber of choice is dog fur, Charilyn is quick to note that not all breeds of dogs have the right stuff.

"I don't like to spin it if the individual fiber is under an inch and a half in length. So longhaired dogs like Newfoundlands are great . . . I love to spin Newfoundlands, Samoyeds, Shelties . . . and I just finished an order for a longhaired Akita. To look at one, you wouldn't think it would be fun to spin, but this one was gorgeous. You can do huskies, and, of course, my Old English Sheepdogs. I've done many, many different breeds."

Most of Charilyn's customers prefer their dog-fur yarn pure, with no other fibers blended in. But there are certain drawbacks, she says.

"It doesn't have a lot of elasticity, like wool. And sweaters made of dog fur are really, really hot. It's more like an outside jacket. I'd rather use the dog fur as a decoration or embellishment in the sweater. But when you're walking, or doing other outdoor activities during Alaska winters, there is nothing like dog-fur mittens to keep your hands warm.

But does the finished product smell like a dog?

"That's the one thing that everybody wants to know. People say, 'Oh, I've smelled dog-fur yarn and it smells awful!' Well, if it smells bad, then they haven't cleaned it properly.

"Dog fur is much like angora," Charilyn adds. "It is always going to shed some, but the shedding will diminish as it's worn. It's very soft. Some of it is just absolutely gorgeous. And why not recycle dog fur? Not only will you have a beautiful garment, but lasting memories of a furry friend." ∎

Charilyn spins the dog fur (or other exotic fiber) on a traditional Ashford spinning wheel. *(Photo by Nancy Gates)*

Recycling Dog Fur

PEOPLE SAY, "I have all kinds of hair; it just comes out in clumps!" But you need to look at each individual fiber to see how long it really is. I like an inch and a half.

I have an electric drum carder, which I use if there's a lot of fiber. If a person wants the colors separate, then I'll use my hand cards. Carding separates and straightens the fibers. After I card it, I spin it.

Spinning the fibers involves twisting them into one continuous strand, using a spinning wheel or a drop spindle. I use a traditional, Ashford wheel. I spin the fiber dirty. I've tried to wash it before I spin it, but you can't agitate it at all, because it tends to mat . . . So I spin it dirty, then I ply singles into a two-ply yarn of about 120 yards per skein.

Once it's in a skein, I just wash it, and wash it and wash it in the sink—in really hot water—until all the dirt is out. I pick up the skein and put it back in, getting the water worked all the way through it. Then I pick it back up again. By that time the water is so dirty that I'll have to do it again with clean water. And I just keep doing it. Sometimes I wash it, maybe, ten times in very hot water and Ivory Snow Powder. There should be no odor. You can use a little bit of vinegar in your last rinse; that will cut any odor that's left.

Then I squeeze it out and put it in a towel to get rid of as much moisture as possible. I dry it by actually putting it on a warping reel for blocking, which sets the twist and places the same tension on every strand. You can also do that, to some extent, by hanging it on a shower curtain rod and then putting some kind of weight on it.

—*Charilyn Cardwell*

Not all breeds of dogs have fur that works well for spinning. Fibers must be at least 1½ inches in length. Longhaired breeds like Newfoundlands, Samoyeds, Shelties, Akita, and Old English Sheepdogs all have the "right stuff" for spinning purposes.

42 How to Build an Icehouse
GALE and JEAN VAN DIEST, Holikachuk, Grayling
Alaskan since 1954

Gale and Jean Van Diest boarded a plane for Alaska on their baby's first birthday, making it an easy date to remember nearly sixty years later. After an initial summer spent in Seward, on the Kenai Peninsula, the little family was sent out as missionaries to the remote Athabascan village of Holikachuk—population 125—on the Innoko River in Western Alaska. During their years in Holikachuck, and later Grayling, they learned how to survive in the wilderness, without electricity or running water, from the local Natives, who became their close friends and mentors.

Above, right: Gale and Jean Van Diest, along with their infant son, boarded a plane some sixty years ago and flew to their new home in the remote Athabascan village of Holikachuk, population 125. *(Photo courtesy Gale Van Diest)*

Above, left: Holikachuk was located on the Innoko River in Western Alaska. Gale and Jean learned how to survive in the Alaska wilderness, without electricity or running water, from local Native mentors and friends. This photo is of Holikachuk in the mid-1950s, taken at 50 degrees below zero. *(Photo courtesy Gale Van Diest)*

The Van Diests weren't strangers to hard work, but among their many new skills were how to hunt, drive dog teams, trap, and skin.

Gale was born to a farming family in northern Washington. His father eventually entered mission work, and founded the Portland Rescue Mission, still in operation today. Jean's mother was a nurse; her father, an "entrepreneur" who had served as a WWI medic, directed a hospital, worked as an X-ray technician, and labored as a journeyman electrician, and a carpenter.

"I remember my father saying, 'If a human being made it, I can fix it.' And he essentially did that," Jean says.

In Holikachuk, Gale and Jean wore many hats and reaped the benefits of their parents' can-do examples and instruction. Gale had some limited medical training in preparation for the mission field, so he became the village's medical aide. Jean drew on her experience as the daughter of a medic and a nurse to lend a competent hand.

"We had radio contact with a doctor at the hospital in Bethel," Gale recalls. "And the doctor kept a schedule every evening, so if I had something I didn't know how to handle, I'd call him, and he'd say, 'Give a shot of penicillin.'

"I used butterfly bandages for cuts that didn't require stitches; if they really had to have stitches, we sent them out to get professional care. But I did a lot of injections. I pulled teeth. I had just enough dental training to make me dangerous," he quips.

Five of the couple's six children were born in Alaska. Sadly, their second child, a son, died in Holikachuk when he was eighteen months old, a victim of Asian flu.

Like other Bush Alaska residents, Gale hunted and fished to keep food on the table. Jean ordered staple groceries, which were delivered by barge from Seattle on a yearly basis. They had no running water at either village site. In Holikachuk, they collected buckets of drinking water from rain that fell on the galvanized roof of the grocery store. In wintertime, Gale would cut "beautiful, clear two-foot-square chunks of ice" from the slough behind the village, haul them home by dogsled, and store them in a fifty-gallon barrel behind the house. These ice blocks were then melted to provide drinking water.

Top: The Van Diests moved to Holikachuk primarily to serve as missionaries, but Gene soon became the village medical aide and also stayed busy hunting, fishing, and hauling water to provide for their growing family. The main trail through the village is shown in the above picture, with the *kashim* (Native meeting hall) on the right. *(Photo courtesy Gale Van Diest)*

Bottom: The village of Holikachuk flooded frequently in the spring. The boat in the above photo, located at the Van Diest's front door, was a typical riverboat that the men of the village helped Gale build. Beyond the boat is the village's log chapel. *(Photo courtesy Gale Van Diest)*

"We had no electricity and no refrigeration. In the summertime, it gets kind of hot up there in the Interior—up to 85 or 90 degrees," he remembers.

Gale eventually built the family's icehouse for a cool place to store perishables in Holikachuk's hot summers. By stacking the blocks of ice in the cool, underground icehouse, he also provided a ready supply of water in summer or winter.

The Van Diest family lived in Holikachuk for eight years, and when they did decide to move, it was because the entire village moved.

"The village would flood from time to time," Gale explains. There was not a good source for drinking water, and since every summer practically the whole village would travel a full day by boat—through a long slough—to fish camps on the Yukon River, the decision was made to move the village to that area."

In 1960, village leaders chose to relocate to a site where Grayling Creek joined the Yukon River.

For two winters all the village men traveled by dog team to a wooded area along the Yukon, where they cut logs and hauled them to the riverbank. In the spring of 1962, these logs were made into rafts and floated down the river to the new village site of Grayling where they were made into lumber. Some assistance was given by a number of government agencies, but local men did most of the work.

Today, seemingly unable to retire—the Van Diests split their time between Washington State and Alaska's Matanuska Valley, where Gale serves as acting director for InterAct Ministries. Gale and Jean also enjoy spending time there with their Alaskan grandchildren—three of their sons still live in the area and are raising their families there. ■

Put It on Ice

FOR AN ICEHOUSE, you have to dig down into the ground. The hole has to be pretty big; mine was eight feet wide, and maybe twelve feet long, and about six feet down into the ground. I used my tractor.

I built walls with slabs from an old sawmill, bark-side out, so the inside walls would be smooth, then backfilled the soil—like you would a foundation.

The top of the icehouse was just visible above ground. The roof was made of boards, and covered first with tarpaper, then with soil—to help insulate it.

Then I hauled lots of sawdust—enough to cover the floor with about eight to ten inches, built a door, and cut some steps into the ground going down to it. All this was done during the summer.

When the local slough froze over, I cut big, clear, two-foot-square chunks of ice and hauled them home in my dogsled.

I stacked the ice blocks on the back half of the icehouse floor—two or three lines at first—then covered them with plenty of sawdust, then put another layer on top, covered it with sawdust, and continued adding layers until I reached the top—about five or six feet. Then I did the same thing for the front half [of the floor]. We didn't need a drain, because the ice didn't melt.

We boiled our drinking water. That was the craziest part. In winter, we'd bring ice in, melt it, boil it, and put it out on the back porch to cool. Then we'd forget it, and it would freeze again!

—*Gale and Jean Van Diest*

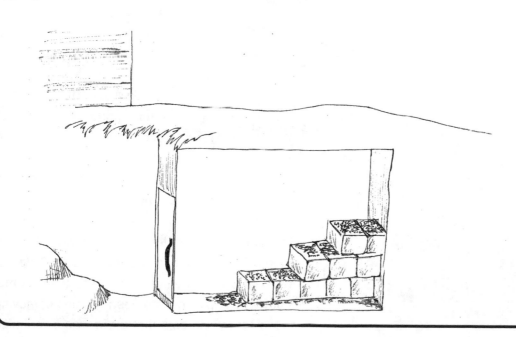

43 How to Run a Trapline

KEITH ROWLAND, McCarthy
Alaska-born in 1964

Keith Rowland loves life in McCarthy, a little town of about fifty people who have chosen to live in Alaska's scenic Copper River Valley. He appreciates the closeness of the mountains and glaciers, and the general "wildness" of the country. There, in a log home set on 160 acres at the confluence of the Kennicott and Nizina Rivers, Keith and his wife, Laurie, are raising their five kids.

Keith himself grew up in a cozy log cabin home, too, back in the soft folds of the Matanuska Valley, about an hour north of Anchor-

Top: Keith Rowland learned about trapping in Alaska, ". . . mostly through books and through trial and error."
(Photo by Nancy Gates)

Bottom: Woverine pelt. *(Photo by Nancy Gates)*

age. His mother, Nancy, is a retired schoolteacher and an avid quilter, and his father, Kenneth, a lifelong Alaskan, spent his working life as a welder and machinist for the coal mines around Healy. Now retired, Kenneth has more time for hunting and fishing. Keith's interests, however, focused on trapping.

"My dad loves to hunt. But for some reason, I just picked trapping," Keith says. "He'd come along because he was interested in critters and whatnot. I learned about trapping mostly through books and through trial and error."

As a youngster, Keith put his newly acquired book knowledge to work by running traplines around his home, trapping whatever he could find. The Rowland family made frequent recreational trips to the McCarthy area. Years later, when Keith grew up and married his best friend's sister, he and Laurie decided to make McCarthy their home.

"We were interested in three different 'Recreational Parcels' of land," he remembers. "We visited all three sites one summer, and then we met a guy who told us he had been thinking of moving to McCarthy. He said that there was a real nice

Leghold traps on display
at Keith's parents' cabin.
(Photos by Nancy Gates)

property there where the rivers meet, but he couldn't figure out how to get a road to it, so he didn't go. That instantly clicked in my mind; I knew that I'd really like that piece of property. So we came right out here, found the owners, and bought the land. And that's where we live today."

Keith managed to "figure out" how to get a road into his new McCarthy property. In fact, he now owns a construction company, Rowcon, which specializes in road and driveway construction. Laurie keeps the books for the business and homeschools the children; Keith teaches them to trap.

"We have a family trapline," he says. "In fact, the homeschooling is tailored around it. Laurie teaches Monday through Thursday. Then the older boys have a three-day weekend. We go out on our main trapline—about 140 miles long—on Friday morning, overnight, and then trap all day

Saturday. Then we're back for church on Sunday."

The Rowlands run other lines that range from two to thirty miles long. Keith and his two older sons run the longer traplines with snowmachines.

"They own theirs," Keith says, "and they buy their own gas out of money they earn by trapping during the winter and doing odd jobs during the summer."

The shorter traplines can be checked after school from the house, and Keith's twelve-year-old son walks some of those lines. Occasionally his sister joins him.

And what kinds of animals are they trapping?

"Our emphasis is martens, wolverines, and lynx—when they're around, but lynx are cyclical. We also get some beavers, mink, a few coyotes, and a few fox. We try for wolves, but we don't catch very many of them because they're pretty scarce in our area."

Keith sells his upper-end wolverine furs to friends or to taxidermists. Most of his remaining furs go to a Canadian company that acquires thousands of furs and sells them at auction. After taking a percentage of the sale price, the balance of the proceeds is sent back to the trappers. ■

Smaller leghold trap for martens, lynx, or coyotes.
(Photo by Nancy Gates)

THE ALASKA TRAPPERS ASSOCIATION is a great organization that is really helpful when somebody is starting to trap. There are actually several chapters; the main one is in Fairbanks. They hold a two-day trappers school every year. Experienced trappers come in and tell you about their specialty. Topics include how to trap, how to maintain a snowmachine, how to camp in the cold—just about everything you'll need to know. I highly recommend interested people to go to that.

Then find out who traps where you live, or where you are planning to trap. Strike up a friendship with him and try to go with him on his lines. Also, nowadays there are many good how-to books on the subject.

In Alaska, any state land is open to trapping and cannot be set aside for just one individual. Theoretically, you can go right down somebody's trapline and trap right beside him or her; but ethically, you don't do it that way. The Alaska Trappers Association has a code of ethics that should be followed.

Basically, we use three kinds of traps. We generally use leghold traps for martens and lynx and sometimes for coyotes and wolves. We use snares for beavers, but occasionally we also use those for lynx and wolves, as well. A conibear is a body-gripping trap that's supposed to kill quickly and humanely; we use them to trap wolverines.

Getting Started Trapping

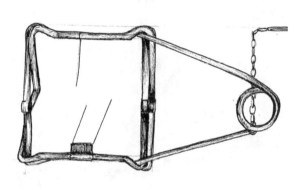

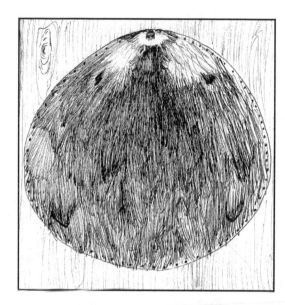

For wolverines, Keith uses a body-gripping, conibear trap; for beavers (and occasionally lynx and wolves), he uses snares.

Once we trap the animal, we skin it and nail the pelt onto a wooden board to dry, with the skin-side out. Beavers are stretched onto a four-foot-square piece of plywood—round, like a silver dollar. Everything else is stretched over a long, skinny board that is roughly shaped like the animal. We stretch them about a day or so until the skin gets a little tacky, and then turn them, putting the fur-side out to finish drying. After about a week, we take them off the board and put them on wire hangers.

We either sell the beaver meat to dog mushers, or use it in our traps—everything likes to eat beaver meat. Lynx meat tastes really good, but we catch too many to eat them all; some we give away and some we use for bait. Lynx meat reminds me a little bit of . . . chicken.

—*Keith Rowland*

44 How to Survive Alaska Winters in a Tent

KEN DEARDORFF, McGrath
Alaskan since 1973

In a book about homesteader skills, it's only fitting that the last chapter features the last person to receive land under the Homestead Act of 1862. Ken Deardorff, a twenty-nine-year-old Vietnam veteran from Southern California, filed for his homestead land along the Stony River, near McGrath, in 1974. He had fulfilled all the Homestead Act requirements by 1979, but did not actually receive his patent until May of 1988, giving him the distinction of being America's—and Alaska's—last homesteader.

Ken was raised in Monrovia, California. His father was a truck driver and his mother a homemaker. Ken says he had learned about homesteading in Alaska when he was a child by reading outdoor magazines. He dreamed of living in Alaska someday; in 1973, he made that dream a reality.

"I had decided, when I was about seven years old, that I hated California and wanted to live in Alaska. So after I got out of college, I decided that this was the time to go."

Ken's first stop was in Anchorage, where he spent several days at the Bureau of Land Management office poring over maps and aerial photographs of the areas of Alaska that were open and available for homesteading.

"After careful consideration, I finally decided on the spot where I wanted to be dropped off—along the Stony River."

Ken's future homestead was located about

In May of 1988, Ken Deardorff, a twenty-nine-year-old Vietnam veteran from Southern California, officially became Alaska's—and America's—last homesteader under the Homestead Act of 1862. *(Photo courtesy Ken Deardorff)*

200 air miles northwest of Anchorage, deep in Alaska's Interior. Ken recalls that he was required to clear ⅛ of the total acreage, cultivate it, build a habitable dwelling, and live there for at least thirty-six months. He first lived on the land in a nylon tent while he built a small cabin.

"I lived right there in a cabin I built. I fished, hunted, gardened, and trapped like all real Americans should," he says, smiling. "And I also cleared land—seemingly forever."

Ken faced many challenges while living his dream. One challenge he says he and his daughter, Susan, will never forget happened one February morning in 1979 with they were out checking traps.

"It was about ten below and I was snowshoeing and pulling three-year-old Susan behind me in a little plastic sled. We were enjoying the time outside and watching all the different tracks in the snow. About a hundred yards ahead of us, a moose came out of the brush—toward us—at a trot. I grabbed Susan from the sled and set her up in the forks of a large birch tree. I was armed only with my old .22 rifle, so the moose and I played Mexican standoff around another tree until she finally lost interest and wandered off. No one was hurt, and no shots fired, but both Susan and I still remember that day as though it was yesterday."

Ken and his family lived in their cabin by the Stony River for about ten years. He later sold the property and moved into McGrath. His daughter now lives with two daughters of her own in Fairbanks. Both Ken and his daughter have many fond memories of their rustic lives at Stony River.

"We definitely miss it, both me and my daughter. No phone, no neighbors, no noise. I'd always wanted to live in a place I could just raise the window and shoot something. I certainly got that, in spades. It was an exciting life, and if I could change anything, I think I would do just more of the same."

While many of Ken's wilderness experiences were difficult and even dangerous, the rewards of that lifestyle, in his mind at least, far outweighed the hardships. He coped by learning a variety of essential backcountry skills, like how to survive an Alaska winter in a tent. ■

Winter Camping in Alaska

I HAVE SPENT A LOT of time in a tent during the winter. It can be pleasant or miserable, depending on the tent and your preparation.

In my opinion, a canvas wall tent is the only way to go. A small woodstove with good, dry wood will keep things toasty and give you a place to cook, sleep, eat, skin furbearers, and dry your wet clothes.

It is important to cover your tent with a fly made from a vinyl tarp or just plastic sheeting. This really helps hold in the heat and keeps outside sparks from burning a hole in the roof.

It's a good idea to use small spruce boughs between the canvas and the tarp to keep condensation from wicking into the tent. It will also prevent mildew on the canvas.

A tent fly made from a vinyl tarp or plastic sheeting helps insulate the tent. Adding a layer of small spruce boughs between the tent and the fly keeps condensation from wicking into the tent, and mildew from forming on the tent.

Winter Camping in Alaska (cont'd)

For light, Ken usually uses a Coleman lantern hanging from the ridgepole of the tent by a string and a forked stick.

For light, I usually use a Coleman lantern. I hang it from the ridgepole of the tent with a string and a forked stick. The stick is like the letter Y, and a string is tied to one short leg of the stick and then to the ridge. Hang the lantern from the other branch of the Y.

—*Ken Deardorff*

The plastic or tarp helps snow slide off the top and automatically bank against the sides of the tent to help hold more heat. Be sure the bottom edge of the canvas wall is turned in rather than out. This will prevent freezing down.

If you are pitching your tent when there is already a lot of snow, shovel the snow away from the stove area; it will turn into a mud hole if you don't. Pile the snow into the rear area where you will sleep. Also stack cut spruce bows in your sleeping area, and then cover with a tarp, preferably canvas. This is your bed. A caribou hide is a wonderful insulator to put under your sleeping bag.

I prefer NOT sleeping on a cot, as it allows cold air to circulate underneath you.

Finally, be sure to make shavings and kindling before you go to sleep. I like to be able to reach the stove door from my sleeping bag so I don't have to get up to light a new fire. Make it right from bed and snooze some more while the coffee heats up.

Ken Deardorff believes that a canvas wall tent is the only good option for comfortable winter camping in Alaska. A small woodstove with an ample supply of dry wood will keep you warm and provide space for cooking, sleeping, eating, and working. A pile of snow topped with spruce bows, a canvas tarp, and then a caribou hide makes a good platform for your sleeping bag.

ACKNOWLEDGMENTS

Thank you husbands, Perry Brown and Chris Gates, for your kindness, patience, and meal-time resourcefulness. To Linda Nelson, for transcription help and consistent encouragement. To Jessi Gates, for her helpful spirit and technical expertise, and to Natalie Gates for sharing her artistic talents.

Our thanks to Doug Pfeiffer, Tim Frew, Kathy Howard, and Vicki Knapton for helping to hammer this book into shape.

And to each of our "homesteaders," who gave us their time, shared their knowledge, and gathered useful photos and drawings, our warmest thanks. Many people went to great lengths to help with referrals, materials, and fact-checking, and should receive special acknowledgment, including Ole Wik, Charlie Lean, Teena Helmericks, John Binkley, Mary Binkley, Joel Doner, Becky and Rene Contreras, Mark Ausdahl, Rose Hurst, Dave Ward, Leigh Thorson, Ken and Nancy Rowlands, Lori Mumford, Fred and Carolyn Harding, and Carla Merriner.

Several elders have passed away since we began researching this book, among them R. N. DeArmond, who served as a wonderful advisor. We also said farewell to Alaska pioneers Harmon "Bud" Helmericks, Clarence Bakk, Douglas Colp, Marlin Grasser, Dr. Charles Manwiller, and Maxine DeVilblss, each of whom contributed enormously to the shaping of a state as well as to the success of this book.

READING LIST

Alaska Northwest Books. *Alaska Wild Berry Guide and Cookbook.* Portland, Ore.: Alaska Northwest Books, 1983.

Allman, Ruth. *Alaska Sourdough Cookbook.* Portland, Ore.: Alaska Northwest Books, 2003.

Brown, Tricia. *The World-Famous Alaska Highway: A Guide to the Alcan and Other Wilderness Roads of the North,* 4th ed. Golden, Col.: Fulcrum Publishing, 2011.

_____, ed. *The Iditarod Fact Book,* 2nd edition. Kenmore, Wash.: Epicenter Press, 2006.

Clark, Dexter and Lynette *"Yukon Yonda." On Golden Ground: Our Journey to the Eldorado.* Anchorage: Larson & Larrigan, 1997.

Corral, Roy (photographer). *Alaska Native Ways: What the Elders Have Taught Us.* Portland, Ore.: Graphic Arts Books, 2002.

_____. *Portrait of the Alaska Railroad.* Portland, Ore.: Alaska Northwest Books, 2003.

Fields, Leslie Leyland. *Out on the Deep Blue: True Stories of Daring, Persistence, and Survival from the Nation's Most Dangerous Profession.* New York: St. Martin's Griffin, 2002.

_____. *Surviving the Island of Grace: A Life on the Wild Edge of America.* Kenmore, Wash.: Epicenter Press, 2008.

Frederic, Lisa. *Running with Champions: A Midlife Journey on the Iditarod Trail.* Portland, Ore.: Alaska Northwest Books, 2006.

Fredston, Jill A. and Doug Fesler. *Snow Sense: A Guide to Evaluating Snow Avalanche Hazard.* Anchorage: Alaska Mountain Safety Center, 1999.

_____. *Rowing to Latitude: Journeys along the Arctic's Edge.* New York: North Point Press, 2002.

_____. *Snowstruck: In the Grip of Avalanches.* San Diego, Calif.: Harcourt, 2005.

Gates, Nancy, ed. *The Alaska Almanac: Alaska's Favorite Factbook,* 33rd ed. Portland, Ore.: Alaska Northwest Books, 2011.

Helmericks, Harmon. *The Last of the Bush Pilots: Flying the Alaskan Wilderness.* Crabtree, Ore.: Narrative Press, 2008. First hardcover edition published by Alfred Knopf, 1969.

Kantner, Seth. *Shopping for Porcupine: A Life in Arctic Alaska*. Minneapolis: Milkweed Editions, 2008.

_____. *Ordinary Wolves*. Minneapolis: Milkweed Editions, 2004.

King, Jeff. *Cold Hands, Warm Heart: Alaskan Adventures of an Iditarod Champion*, 2nd ed. Denali Park, Alaska: Husky Homestead, Inc., 2011.

Marsh, Ken. *Breakfast at Trout's Place: The Seasons of an Alaskan Flyfisher*. Boulder, Col.: Johnson Books, 1999.

Miller, Orlando. *The Frontier in Alaska and the Matanuska Colony*. New Haven, Conn.: Yale University Press, 1975.

Orth, Joy. *Island: Our Alaskan Dream and Reality*. Portland, Ore.: Alaska Northwest Books, 1987.

Pratt, Verna. *Alaska's Wild Berries*. Anchorage: Alaskrafts Publishing, 1995.

_____. *Field Guide to Alaskan Wildflowers*. Anchorage: Alaskrafts Publishing, 1991.

_____. *Wildlflowers of Denali National Park*. Anchorage: Alaskrafts Publishing, 1993.

Roberts, Ann D. *Alaska Gardening Guide*. Anchorage: Publication Consultants, 2000.

Runyan, Joe. *Winning Strategies for Distance Mushers*. Cliff, N.M.: Desert Hound Publishing Co., 2003.

Simpson, Sherry. *The Accidental Explorer: Wayfinding in Alaska*. Seattle: Sasquatch Books, 2008.

_____. *The Way Winter Comes: Alaska Stories*. Seattle: Sasquatch Books, 1998.

Viereck, Eleanor. *Alaska Wilderness Medicines: Healthful Plants of the Far North*, 6th ed. Portland, Ore.: Alaska Northwest Books, 1987.

Walker, Tom. *Building the Alaska Log Home*. Kenmore, Wash.: Epicenter Press, 2007.

_____. *Kantishna: Mushers, Miners, Mountaineers: The Pioneer Story Behind Mount McKinley National Park*. Missoula, Mont.: Pictorial Histories Publishing, 2006.

Wik, Ole. *Wood Stoves: How to Make and Use Them*. Portland, Ore.: Alaska Northwest Books, 1977.

INDEX

Page locators in *italics* refer to photographs.